The Louisiana Purchase

An American Story

The Louisiana Purchase

An American Story

John Chase

Foreword by Emilie Dietrich Griffin

PELICAN PUBLISHING COMPANY
Gretna 2002

For Alyssa and Trina

First published by Habersham Corporation
Published by arrangement with Habersham Corporation by
  Pelican Publishing Company, Inc., 2002

First Pelican edition, 2002

---

*The word "Pelican" and the depiction of a pelican are trademarks
of Pelican Publishing Company, Inc., and are registered in the
U.S. Patent and Trademark Office.*

Library of Congress Cataloging-in-Publication Data

Chase, John Churchill.
    The Louisiana Purchase : an American story / John Chase. -- 1st
Pelican ed.
        p.   cm.
    Summary: A history of the events leading to, surrounding, and
resulting from the Louisiana Purchase, presented in the form of a
comic book.
    ISBN 1-58980-084-2 (pbk. : alk. paper)
    1. Louisiana Purchase--Juvenile literature.   [1. Louisiana
Purchase--Cartoons and comics. 2. Cartoons and comics.]   I. Title.
E333.C49 1998
973.4'6--dc21   98-50322
                                                                  CIP
                                                                   AC

Design by Wayne Miller

Printed in the United States of America

Published by Pelican Publishing Company, Inc.
1000 Burmaster Street, Gretna, Louisiana 70053

AMERICA'S BEST BUY
THE LOUISIANA PURCHASE
by CHARLES NUTTER

The Louisiana Purchase in 1803 was the third greatest event in American History, ranking directly behind the Declaration of Independencec and the framing of the Constitution. It doubled the size and multiplied many times the power of the struggling young American republic, and completely changed its history since it meant the inevitable expansion to the shores of the Pacific and domination of North America by free, liberty-loving and progressive people who were united.

The Purchase was America's greatest diplomatic triumph, the greatest, strangest real estate bargain in all history. It meant the beginning of the end of Colonialism in the New World, and paved the way for the Monroe Doctrine. It established the struggling United States as a world power and factor for peace. It was a great milestone in history, significant far beyond present day knowledge of the event.

As he laying in exile in the spring of 1821 Napoleon Bonaparte was inclined to let his mind wander back through the incredible adventures of his life. At one stage he remarked:

> "If I had the choice, I would go to America. I would pay a visit to Louisiana. After all it was I who gave it to the Americans."

The vast unknown territory west of the Mississippi River was a problem and a financial drain on European nations so long as it remained a colony. It had been so for two and half centuries until the Americans acquired this area in 1803. Within a very short period after all, its real opportunity and resources began to be exploited. Soon, even the most bitter skeptics discovered that we had stumbled into the greatest real estate bargain in all history, when we acquired this area of some 900,000 square miles of territory at about four cents an acre.

The men who foresaw the significance of the acquisition of this territory and who carried it out in the face of antagonistic public opinion for the most part are amongthe greatest heroes of American history. Robert R. Livingston takes his place at the top of this list,

along with President Thomas Jefferson, James Madison and James Monroe, the latter three of whom served their time as Presidents of the United States.

Suddenly presented the opporunity to acquire an area roughly as large at that already possessed by the United States for 15 million dollars, Livingston and Monroe negotiated the Purchase without authority, without money and without any idea of the exact boundaries of the territory they were purchasing. They feared that the Purchase would have a bad reaction in the United States and be vigorously opposed by political enemies. They knew it would be extremely difficult to raise the money to pay Napoleon. They knew they lacked any sembelance of authority to proceed, but they also knew that this was the opportunity that could not be passed by. Jefferson, after the original shock, saw the same facts and puched the Purchase through to ratification despite the Constutional arguments raised against it. Even so, it passed Congress by less than a handful of votes. Had the opposition prevailed the Treaty would have moved in and taken over the Louisiana Purchase area, which at that time was wholly unprotected.

Briefly, the facts of the Louisiana Purchase follow:

On May 1, 1541 De Soto discovered the Mississippi River near Helena, Arkansas, and Coronado, moving from Mexico, discovered the Missouri River somewhere north of St. Joseph, Missouri. He was greatly impressed by the countless buffalo which he called crooked back Oxen.

Thier discoveries were lost for 130 years until on June 1673 Marquette and Joliet came west from Montreal and found the Mississippi River again, west of Chicago.They were the first Frenchmen who ever saw it, and they followed the river down to Arkansas. They called it the St. Louis, the Missouri, the St. Philip and the Ohio La Belle. Incidentally, Lake Fort Ponchartrain was the first settlement and founding of Detroit.

In 1682 La Salle named the central area of the United States, Louisiana, and claimed it for France.

The original Louisiana consisted of the entire territory drained by the Mississippi River and all of its tributaries, and the area in southeastern United States lying east of the Mississippi River watershed and north of the Palm River, a small stream in central western Florida on Sarasota Bay. This origianl area consisted of approximately two-thirds of the United States as we know it today, and was made up of all or parts of thirty-one states spread from New york, Pennsylvania, Maryland and Viginia westward to Idaho and Montana.

The Louisiana area never flowered under either France or Spain, and indeed was a financial headache and drain to both countries throughout the two and a half centuries they controlled it. Govenor General Cadillac looked the place over and told Crozat that

"This whole continent is not worth having."

In 1762 France had ceded Louisiana to Spain in a secret treaty the terms of whihch did not become known and published for seventy years. Spain did nothing of consequence to develop the territory other than occupation of New Orleans. Napoleon coerced Spain to cede it back to France in another secret treaty, called the Treaty of San Idlephonso, in 1800.

This treaty did not become effective until ratification and its very existence was denied at Madrid and Paris for nearly two years. In the meantimes, however, we had become embroiled in serious trouble with both Spain and France, which were inclined to disregard the newly won rights of the American Rebuplic.

At sea we had been engaged in two years of cold war with French raiders who had been attacking our ships even back since the President Washington administration, and a large claim for spoilation had piled up against France.

In 1795 the United States has succeeded in getting a five year treaty with Spain giving the United States the right of deposit at New Orleans which was essential to settlement of the western area of the thirteen colonies. The right of barges and ships to exchange their cargoes at the mouth of the Mississippi River was essential to the development of mis-United States, and this was recognized from the beginning. It was stated and understood that New Orleans was the key to the Mississippi and the Mississippi Valley and that must either be in the hands of the United States or a nation friendly to us if we were ever to develop middle-America.

"There is on the globe one single spot, the posession of which is our natural and habitual enemy—that being New Orleans."

President Jefferson made this somewhat bellicose, certainly decisive statement to Robert R. Livingston, Minister to France, at one stage of the Purchase negotiations, and other time he stated

"from the moment that France takes possession of New Orleans we must marry ourselves to the British fleet and nation."

We were at that stage ready to join our late enemy the British in order to get New Orleans. Spanish mistakes helped to chrystallize the situation for in 1802 the Spanish intendant Morales suspended the now-lapsed deposit rights, inflaming talk of war. Congress spent weeks discussing an appropriation of five million dollars and raising of an army to move on New Orleans and seize it.

"We must know at once whether we can acquire New Orleans or not. We are satisfied nothing else will secure us against a war. The future destinies of our country hang on the event of this negotiation."

These forceful, prophetic words were delivered by President Jefferson during the negoiation that Living ston had initiated in Paris for New Orleans.

President Thomas Jefferson came into office in 1801 and within the year he had dispatched Livingston to Paris as Minister with instructions to clarify the situation at New Orleans by blocking if he could the retrocession of Louisiana to France, by convincing the French that the city of New Orleans and the Floridas were valueless to them and should be given to the united States, to get permanent rights of deposit or, if possible, to buy the city of New Orleans. A Congressional grant of $2,000,000 was made for the latter purpose.

At this jucture, the United States would have settled for the permanent right for joint use of New Orleans for transshipment of river and ocean commerce.

Before Livingston could reach Paris, however, France and England signed the Peace of Amiens and Napoleon appointed General Victor Emmanual LeClerc, his-brother-in-law, to head an expedition to Haiti to suppress the independence movement there, and thence to proceed to Louisiana to take over. LeClerc departed in December, 1801 with 45,000 French soldiers and the largest armada that ever left Europe for the new world.

Livngston, on December 30, 1801, told Rufus King, Minister to England, that he had learned that the expedition being sent out to Hispaniola was then to proceed to Louisiana provided the Negro Patriot Toussaint made no opposition.

All during 1802 Livingston worked diligently on his mission, writing memorials, consulting with officials and laying groundwork of opposition to colonization of Louisiana, and attempting to purchase New Orleans and West Florida. In September he told Madison:

"There never was a government in which less can be done by negoiation. There are no people, no legislature, no concillors. One man is everything. His ministers are mere clerks, and his legislators and concillors but parade officers. All reflecting men are opposed to the wild expedition to Louisiana, but no man dares tell Napoleon so."

The principal events of 1802 and the early part of 1803 are herewith summarized:

February5, 1802—King informed Madison of French plans to send an expedition to Louisiana.

February 20, 1802—Livingston requested information from the French governement as to its plans for Louisiana, but was not answered.

February 26, 1802—Livinston informed Madison that french statesmen were opposed to the acquistion of Louisiana, but that it was a "favorite object" with Napoleon.

March 24, 1802—Livingston informed Madison that the French hoped to command the trade of the western states by controlling New Orleans.

May 1, 1802—Madison instructed Livingston to attempt to divert France from her plans for Louisiana, and to learn the price for which New Orleans and the Floridas would be yielded to the United States.

May 28, 1802—Livingston attempted to learn from the Spanish minister in Paris, the Chevalier J. Nicolay d'Azara, the terms of the cession, and asserted the right of the United States to be a party to any convention ceding the free navigation of the Mississippi River.

June 2, 1802—Livingston received no information except the admission that the cession had been made.

August 10—Livingston circulated a memoir to prove that the posession of Louisiana would be politically and commercially disadvantageous to France.

August 16, 1802—general Claude Perrin Victor was appointed to command the French expedition of 3,000 men to Louisiana.

August 31, 1802—Livingston was informed that France would not negotiate on the sale of New Orleans and the Floridas until France took posession of Louisiana.

October 15, 1802—Charles IV of Spain signed an order to deliver Louisiana to France.

October 15, 1802—Madison informed Livingston that the United States was interested only in purchasing New Orleans and the Floridas.

October 16, 1802—Juan Buenaventura Morales, Spanish intendant in New Orleans, suspendedthe right of deposit in New Orleans and kicked the Americans out.

November-December—Wesern colonists began clamoring for war against Spain and seizure of New Orleans, and within sixty days this debate was continued in Congress where a bill was introduced to appropriate $5,000,000 to finance the war.

November 27, 1802—Madison demanded redress from Spain because ther ight of deposit was withheld.

December 2, 1802—General LeClerc died in Haiti. Death knell to the French campaign there.

December 15, 1802—President Thomas Jefferson intimated to Congress that the cession of Louisiana to France might make a change in the foreign relations of the United States necessary.

February 3, 1803—Jefferson urged Livingston to work diligently for the cession of New Orleans to the U.S.

February 14, 1803—Senator Ross of Pennsylvania delivered a flaming speech on the floor of Congress, demanding war and seizure of New Orleans. His bill to raise 50,000 militia to seize and hold New Orleans was debated for a week, tabled by a narrow margin. Report of this debate and its defiance of Napoleon served Livingston well when it reached his hands nearly two months later.

February 18, 1803—Livngston sent madison a memoir which showed that Great Britain would strain every nerve to acquire Louisiana and Florida; and that, if aided by the United States, the resources of France could not prevent that result.

February 23, 1803—James Monroe appointed a minister to france co-jointly with Livingston.

February 28, 1803—Livngston in a letter to Napoleon urged the pledged faith of the French government for the payment of American claims and informed the First Consul of the alarm in the U.S. over the French acquisition of Louisiana by France. Livingston informed Napoleon that France could not gain any permanent advantage from this acquisition and should cede it to the United States.

March 2, 1803—Livingston and Monroe instructed to negotiate the purchase of New Orleans and the Floridas.

March 8, 1803—Monroe set sail for France.

March 26, 1803—Pierre Clement Laussat arrived in New Orleans to prepare for the French occupation.

April 2, 1803—King informed Madison that in the event of war, whihch seemed inevitable, England was determined to occupy New Orleans.

Thus began the crucial month of April, 1803, during which everything was concluded and arranged, even though it took many more months to ratify the transcation, and several years to "sell" the Purchase not only to our own people, but to convince the governments of Great Britain and Spain that the Purchase was legal and must be respected.

Each day made history during this eventful April. Livingston had builded far better than he knew, and coincidental events had set the stage for the final act. LeClerc was dead, Napoleon had lsot Haiti irretrievably, he faced an immediate war with England well knowingthat protection of distant American colonies without great naval forces. He desperately needed money, ha had thought well of the retrocession but some of his ministries had debated earnestly with him against it, probably influenced by Livingston's earnest and convincing propaganda.

April 10th was Easter Sunday. Napoleon was at St. Cloud where he had summoned Count Barbe Marbois and Duc Denis Decres, his Ministers of Finance and Nay and Colonies. After a general review of world events and the French position Napoleon arose, and with all the earnestness of a conqueror, said:

"I am fully sensible of the value of Louisiana, and it was my desire to repair the error of the French diplomatists who abandoned it in 1762. I have scarcely reeived it before I run the risk of losing it; but if I am obliged to give it up, it shall hereafter cost more to those who force me to part with it, than those to whom I yield it. The English have successfully taken from France: Canada, Cape Breton, Newfoundland, Nova Scotia, and the richest portions of Asia. They are engaged in exciting troubles in St. Domingo. They shall not have the Mississippi, which they covet. Louisiana is nothing in comparison with their conquests in all parts of the globe, and yet the jealous they feel at the restoration of this colony to the sovereignty of France, acquaints me with their wish to take possession of it, and it is thus they will begin the war. They have twenty vessels in the Gulf of Mexico, and our affairs in St. Domingo are daily getting worse since the death of LeClerc. The conquest of Louisiana might be easily made, and I have not a moment to lose in putting it out of their reach. I am not sure but what they have already begun an attack upon it. Such a measure *would be in accordance with their habits, and, in their place, I should not wait. I am inclined, in order to deprive them of all prospect of ever possessing it, to cede it to the United States. Indeed, I can hardly say that I shall ced it, for I do not yet possess it, and if I wait but a short time, my enemies may leave nothing but an empty title to grant to the Rebuplic I wish to conciliate. They only ask for one city of Louisiana, but I consider the whole country lost, and I believe that in the hands of this rising power it will be more useful to the political and even the commercial interests of France, than if I should attempt to retain it. Let me have both your opinion on the subject."*

They discussed the measure without decision. Marbois greatly favored the sale; Decres as earnestly opposed it. The Next day Napoleon said to Marbois.

*"The season for deliberation is over. I have determined to renounce Louisiana. I shall not only give up New Orleans, but the whole country without reservation. * * * I do not undervalue Louisiana. * * * I regret parting with it, but I am convinced that it would be jolly to persist in trying to keep it. I commission you, therefore, to negoiate this affair with the envoys of the United States. * * * Were I to regulate my demands by the importance of this territory to the United States, they would be unbounded; but, being obliged to part with it, I shall be moderate in my terms. Still, remember I must have sixty millions of francs for it, and I will not consent to take less."*

Talleyrand likewise opposed the sale, but was first to break the news to Livingston, that day, although casually when Talleyrand said:

"How would you like to buy all of Louisiana?"

The idea startled Livingston who was unprepared for its implications, and he replied the United States sought only to purchase New Orleans. Talleyrand told him to think it over.

Livingston returned to his embassy late that night and in the midnight dispatch to Jefferson and Madison outlined the new development. There was, of course, no rapid means of communication and he knew his dispatch would not be read for forty-five days or more, and he would need to act without awaiting an answer.

(Negotiations continued without delay between Livingston and Monroe for the United States and Count Francois Barbe-Marbois for france. As a young diplomat, Barbe-Marbois had lived for seven years in the United States, had an American wife, and a great love and friendship for America and Americans. He knew every American patriot from Franklin through John Quincy Adams. He spoke English perfectly, believed in the independence movement, wanted the United States to have Louisiana in order to expand. Monroe later said Barbe-Marbois had been liberal, candid, fair and friendly throughout the negotiations. Barbe-Marbois lived to be 91 years old, and had one of the longest public service records in french history. He served France for 68 years in various important jobs.)

Livingston consulted at once with Monroe. They both realized the price, though remarkably low, was still an immense amount for the new United States, that Congress would have to be called upon not only to ratify the treaty but also to raise the money, that no one knew the boundries of the territory under discussion, that they had no authority or mandate to carry out the negotiations, and that it was necessary for union and strength. Thus reinforced morally they proceeded to conclusion of the treaty on April 30, 1803, when it was signed by Livingston, Monroe and Barbe-Marbois.

The price asked was the equivalent of 120 million francs, and the price given was 80 million francs, sixty million cash and absorbtion of 20 million francs or spoilation claims—the total being $15,000,000.

"What are the boundaries?" Livingston asked Talleyrand at one stage of proceedings. "I don't know," Talleyrand replied, and again pleaded ignorance when asked what was being sold. "Do you mean we are to construe this in our own way," Livingston persisted. "I can give you no direction," Talleyrand replied. "You have made a noble bargain for yourselves and I suppose you will make the most of it."

Indeed Talleyrandmade clear he did not even know if France could deliver the territory if it was sold, as Spain still held it in her possession. But Livingston later told Madison:

"I was willing to take it in any form."

Although their fellow Americans were slow to realize significance of their action, Livingston and Monroe were conscious of the greatness of this event when they signed the treaty, and so was Napoleon. At that time Livingston made this statement:

"We have lived long, but this is the noblest work of our whole lives. The treaty which we have just signed has not been obtained by art or dicated by force; equally advantageous to the

two contracting parties, it will change vast solitudes into flourishing districts. From this day the United States takes their place among the powers of the first rank; the English lose all exclusive influences in the affairs of America. Thus one of the principal causes of European rivalries and animosities is about to cease. however, if wars are inevitable, France will hereafter have in the New World a natural friend, that must increase in strength from year to year, and one which cannot fail to become powerful and respected in every sea. The United States will re-establish the maritime rights of all the world, which are now usurped by a single nation. These treaties will thus be a guarantee of peace and concord among commercial states. The instruments which we have just signed will cause no tears to be shed: they prepare ages of hapiness for innumerable benerations of human creatures. The Mississippi and Missouri will see tehm succeed one another, and multiply, truly worthy of the regard and care of Providence, in the bosom of equality, under just laws, freed from the errors of superstitition and the scourges of bad government."

And Napoleon said:

"This accession of territory strengthens forever the power of the United States; and I have just given to England a maritime rival, that will sooner or later humble her pride. The day may come when the cession of Louisiana to the United States shall render the Americans too powerful for the continent of Europe."

Despite strong opposition the treaty was ratified in October, 1803, and the conventions providing the money were approved in Congress in November. John Quincy Adams, who later was to becme president of the United States, opposed ratification. Four more negative votes would ahve killed the treaty and lost the territory, but Jefferson carried the day.

The story of the Louisiana Purchase is one of the greatness of a handful of Americans who had the wisdom and courage to realize ans seize the opportunity before them. They forged a new philosophy of territorial expansion (purchase), and they started the United States on its way to world power. Many of the ideas that made America great can be traced directly to those stirring days of 1803 when we first moved forward toward our present position in the world.

FOREWORD

I didn't like history books much, as a child. I liked books with stories and pictures in them. Especially stories with a lot of conflict and suspense. I thought Alice in Wonderland really hit the nail on the head when she said, "What is the use of a book without pictures and conversations?" So I read stories. With dialogue and pictures. And I loved the funnypapers.

Then one day my mother brought home a book by John Chase, called *40 Cartoons in Wartime*. I sat down and read it cover to cover.

It was World War II in words and pictures: a collection of the best cartoons Chase had drawn for *The New Orleans States* during the war years.

Later on, I came across the same entertaining approach to history in Chase's *Frenchmen, Desire, Good Children*. All those people in the old portraits at the Cabildo came alive. Every street and every corner had a story to tell, and Chase told it. It's not surprising that the book is a classic now.

The Louisiana Purchase was originally drawn as a daily comic strip which ran in 40 newspapers all over the country. Later on it was gathered in book form and went through several editions. Now, as I look at this new edition, I think Chase may actually have created a new form. He's taken a rich vein of Louisiana history, national history, international history—all the political struggles that went into the making of a territory and a nation and a continent, and told it from both a historical and an editorial cartoon viewpoint. Something I haven't ever quite seen done before.

Chase comments on far-off historical events as though they were happening now. He also has a gift for capturing world figures. For Chase, that's part of a philosophy on what editorial cartooning is all about.

"I don't think any politician objects to being caricatured, no matter how roughly you treat him," Chase said in a nationally televised interview.

"A cartoon is really an audience participation thing," Chase believes. In a sense, he thinks, the cartoonist always speaks for the people. Like famous cartoonists before him, Chase has created a character, known informally as the "Little Man," who does that. The voice of the people is very much felt in this series of strips too.

It's a reminder, I think, that editorial cartooning sprang from a political environment in which people are free to voice opinions about the leaders who form their destiny.

It's a habit of mind, and a style, in this book as in all Chase's work. History with pictures, conversations, and a touch of irreverence.

That's my child's eye view of John Churchill Chase. Something of a legend himself in this Louisiana territory. Because he shares his enjoyment of our part in the history of America so well. With every generation.

Emilie Dietrich Griffin
New Orleans, Louisiana

LOUISIANA PURCHASE

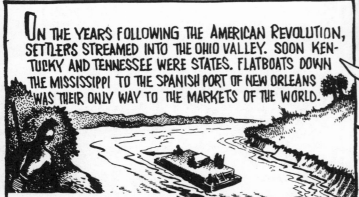  

 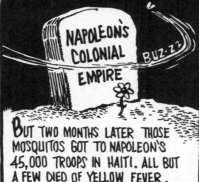 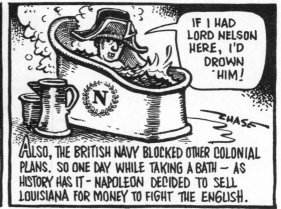

BUT THIS IS A STORY OF MORE THAN A REAL ESTATE DEAL ... MORE THAN HISTORY'S GREATEST REAL ESTATE DEAL .

THIS IS THE STORY OF GREEN PASTURES BEYOND THE WILDEST DREAMS OF DAVID...

IT TELLS OF THE FIRST MEN TO TRAVEL THE STILL WATERS OF ITS VALLEYS — YES, AND TO SURVIVE THE ROUGH WATERS TOO.

IT IS, IN FACT, THE STORY OF MORE THAN HALF OF THE 50 STATES... THAT VAST INLAND THAT LASALLE NAMED **LOUISIANE** —OR "LOUIS' LAND".

An American saga told in that most American of all forms of expression —THE COMIC STRIP!

It's a SPICY STORY ...this Beginning of the New World —and LOUISIANA!

WHY, IT TASTES ALMOST AS GOOD AS IF IT WAS FRESH! HOW DID YOU COOK IT?

WITH SPICE

1300 A.D. - REFRIGERATORLESS EUROPE WAS HAILING A WONDERFUL NEW PRODUCT FROM THE FAR EAST...

IT WILL EVEN MAKE YOUR SANDALS APPETIZING - IN FACT, I HAD MINE FOR BREAKFAST.

SPICE

RETURNING CRUSADERS INTRODUCED SPICE TO EUROPE...

I HOPE I FIND $14,000 WORTH..

CARAVAN ROUTES WERE LONG AND DANGEROUS. SO ALL EUROPEAN NATIONS BEGAN HIRING EXPLORERS TO FIND A SEA ROUTE TO CHINA. SPAIN RISKED $14,000 TO BACK A CAPTAIN NAMED CHRISTOPHER COLUMBUS.

MAKING HISTORY IS VERY CONFUSING.

I PRESUME THIS IS INDIA - SO I NAME YOU INDIAN.

UGH!

IT HAS BEEN WELL SAID THAT COLUMBUS DIDN'T KNOW WHERE HE WAS GOING, AND DIDN'T KNOW WHERE HE HAD BEEN WHEN HE GOT BACK HOME.

HE DIED THINKING HE HAD BEEN TO INDIA.

SPICE-HUNGRY EUROPE DECIDED COLUMBUS HADN'T DISCOVERED ANYTHING BUT A CONTINENTAL ROADBLOCK ACROSS THE WESTERN SEALANES TO THE ORIENT.

I DISCOVERED A PASSAGE AROUND AFRICA.

I DISCOVERED ONE AROUND SOUTH AMERICA.

TOO LONG! I NEED A NORTHWEST PASSAGE.

VASCO DA GAMA

MAGELLAN

EUROPE

? NORTH-WEST PASSAGE ? ? ?

ENGLAND SENT OUT JOHN CABOT. BUT ALL HE DISCOVERED WAS THAT THE FISHING WAS GOOD OFF THE GRAND BANK OF NEWFOUNDLAND. THE KING GAVE CABOT $50 FOR THIS.

I SAVE FIFTY BUCKS.

CABOT SAILED ON A SECOND VOYAGE, BUT NEVER RETURNED.

DON'T YOU WANT TO SEE THE WORLD?

SORRY.. I GOT A DATE.

MEANWHILE IN FRANCE, JACQUES CARTIER RECEIVED ROYAL ORDERS TO MAKE A FRENCH TRY FOR THE NORTHWEST PASSAGE. EXPLORERS HAD DIFFICULTIES SECURING CREWS. CARTIER GOT HIS OUT OF THE JAILS.

THIS **MUST** BE THAT NORTHWEST PASSAGE!

LITTLE IS KNOWN ABOUT **JACQUES CARTIER** ..EXCEPT THAT HE ESTABLISHED FRANCE IN THE NEW WORLD.

ON AUGUST 7, 1535, FEASTDAY OF ST. LAWRENCE, CARTIER DISCOVERED THE GREAT CANADIAN GULF; AND NAMED IT, AND THE RIVER, FOR HIM.

FRANCE SENT HIM ON A SECOND VOYAGE TO EXPLORE MORE, AND ALSO TO CONVERT THE SAVAGES.

MY ORDERS READ THAT YOU'VE GOT TO GO TO CHURCH.

CARTIER EXPLORED THE RIVER ALL THE WAY TO MONTREAL, WHICH HE SO NAMED. (136 YEARS LATER, THE EXPEDITION TO DISCOVER THE MISSISSIPPI WOULD START FROM MONTREAL.)

St. Lawrence — Quebec — Montreal — Ottawa — NOW U.S.A.

CARTIER SAILED HIS SHIP UP THE RIVER, WITH AN INDIAN GUIDE ON BOARD.

KANATA! KANATA! KANATA!

THIS UNKNOWN INDIAN **NAMED** CANADA! HOW IT HAPPENED IS ANOTHER STORY.

KANATA..KANATA.. HM-M, THIS PLACE MUST BE CANADA.

CARTIER'S GUIDE KEPT POINTING TO THE SHORE, REPEATING OVER AND OVER, "KANATA!"

BUT ALL THE GUIDE WAS POINTING OUT WERE THE **WIGWAMS** — IN MOHAWK, THAT'S ABOUT ALL "KANATA" MEANS. SO, THROUGH A MISUNDERSTANDING, CARTIER NAMED THE COUNTRY, "WIGWAM" —OR **CANADA!**

CANADA CLAIMED FOR FRANCE - CARTIER

FOR 75 YEARS FRANCE DID NOTHING ABOUT ITS NEW WORLD LANDS.

ALSO.. SPANISH GALLEONS BEGAN HAULING TREASURE BACK FROM A FABULOUS "SPANISH MAIN". INTEREST IN A NORTH-WEST PASSAGE TO THE ORIENT FADED. SPAIN HAD HIT THE **JACKPOT!**

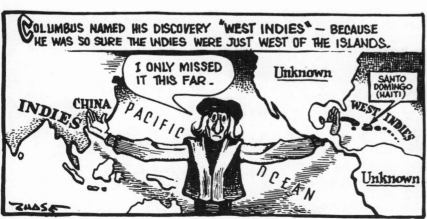

COLUMBUS NAMED HIS DISCOVERY "WEST INDIES" — BECAUSE HE WAS SO SURE THE INDIES WERE JUST WEST OF THE ISLANDS.

I ONLY MISSED IT THIS FAR.

Unknown — CHINA — INDIES — PACIFIC OCEAN — SANTO DOMINGO (HAITI) — WEST INDIES — Unknown

IT WAS FROM BASES IN SANTO DOMINGO IN THESE WEST INDIES THAT SPANISH NAVIGATORS PUSHED WESTWARD... AND FOUND, NOT INDIA, BUT A COLONIAL EMPIRE.

MAYBE I CAN BE LUCKY LIKE SPAIN.

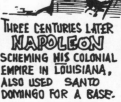

THREE CENTURIES LATER **NAPOLEON** SCHEMING HIS COLONIAL EMPIRE IN LOUISIANA, ALSO USED SANTO DOMINGO FOR A BASE.

EXPLORING IS OFTEN DISGUSTING!

SPANISH CONQUISTADORES LIKE COLUMBUS BEFORE THEM, ALWAYS FOUND **SOMETHING**; BUT THEY NEVER, NEVER FOUND WHAT THEY WENT LOOKING FOR.

...TAKE OLD **PONCE DE LEON**, FOR EXAMPLE—

DOWN IN PUERTO RICO THERE WERE RUMORS OF A **FOUNTAIN OF YOUTH**.. SOMEWHERE NORTHWARD.

DELEON WENT LOOKING FOR IT. HE BATHED IN POOLS ON MOST OF THE 29 BAHAMA ISLANDS, AND ON EASTER SUNDAY IN 1513 HE DISCOVERED AND NAMED **FLORIDA**, WHERE HE ALSO BATHED.

ANYWAY.. I'M THE **CLEANEST** CONQUISTADOR OF THEM ALL.

OLD PONCE FOUND NO FOUNTAIN OF YOUTH — BUT, FOR SPAIN, HE FOUND A FOOTHOLD IN NORTH AMERICA ...

(UNKNOWN) · Florida · WEST INDIES · SPANISH MAINLAND · Mexico · Mayas · Venezuela · Peru

THE FABULOUS **SPANISH MAIN** THAT COLUMBUS THOUGHT WAS THE INDIES TURNED OUT TO BE EVEN RICHER IN 1500 A.D.

YOU'RE TOO UNCIVILIZED TO BE THIS RICH..

IN MEXICO CORTEZ FOUND THE INDIANS ROLLING IN GOLD AND SILVER! IN PERU PIZARRO FOUND MORE OF THE SAME. THE SPANIARDS TOOK IT ALL.

MINES

IT TOOK FIFTY YEARS TO LOOT THE INDIANS OF **ALL** THEIR TREASURES. THEN THE CONQUISTADORES FORCED THEM INTO THE MINES TO DIG UP MORE ...

HERNANDO DESOTO GOT RICH HELPING TO LOOT PERU. HEARING OF MORE GOLD IN FLORIDA, HE DECIDED TO GET RICHER..

ALL I WANT IS MY USUAL ONE FIFTH.

THE KING APPOINTED HIM "CONQUEROR OF FLORIDA" — AT DESOTO'S OWN EXPENSE.

RECRUITS HASTENED TO JOIN THE EXPEDITION, SURE OF BECOMING RICH.

SOME OF US WHO ESCAPED ARE THE ANCESTORS OF EVERY RAZOR-BACK HOG IN THE SOUTH!

ON MAY 28, 1539 DESOTO LANDED NEAR TAMPA BAY WITH 600 MEN. BESIDES SOME HORSES, HE BROUGHT **16 PIGS!** A YEAR LATER HE HAD 300.

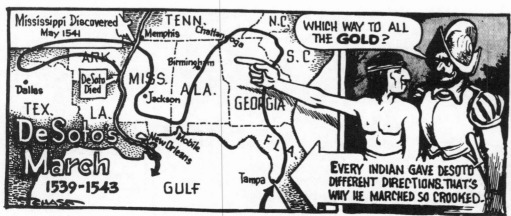

Mississippi Discovered May 1541 · TENN. · Memphis · Chattanooga · N.C. · ARK. · Birmingham · S.C. · DeSoto Died · MISS. · ALA. · Dallas · Jackson · GEORGIA · TEX. · LA. · New Orleans · Mobile · FLA. · Tampa · GULF

DeSoto's March 1539-1543

WHICH WAY TO ALL THE **GOLD**?

EVERY INDIAN GAVE DESOTO DIFFERENT DIRECTIONS. THAT'S WHY HE MARCHED SO CROOKED.

IT SURE IS WIDE.

DESOTO FOUND NO GOLD. INSTEAD HE DISCOVERED THE RICHEST RIVER VALLEY THE WORLD HAS EVER KNOWN .... RICHER THAN ALL THE GOLD THERE IS. HOW IRONIC THAT DESOTO DIED A DISAPPOINTED MAN!

IN PERU, IN MEXICO, THE SPANIARDS HAD TRULY HIT THE JACKPOT. A NEW SPANISH CITY OF MEXICO REPLACED THE NATIVE TOWN, AND BECAME THE CAPITAL OF NEW SPAIN. ONLY FORTY YEARS AFTER COLUMBUS, SPAIN WAS RICH!

SPAIN

YOU WERE A FAIRY TALE—BUT NOT ME!

KING MIDAS

BUT ALAS, SPANIARDS BEGAN TO THINK EVERYTHING THEY TOUCHED IN THIS AMERICA WOULD TURN TO GOLD.

GOLD! NORTH OF MEXICO... SEVEN CITIES OF IT WITH GOLD ROOFS!!

BUT MAYBE, BECAUSE PERU AND MEXICO HAD BEEN SO UNBELIEVABLE, THEY BELIEVED EVERY COCK-AND-BULL STORY OF MORE TREASURE. THEY BELIEVED DE VACA, SOLE SURVIVOR OF AN ILL-FATED EXPEDITION TO FLORIDA, WHO WALKED BACK TO MEXICO.

I WONDER HOW DE SOTO IS DOING? HE LEFT LAST YEAR.

WE OUGHT TO EAT BETTER. BESIDES PIGS, WE GOT GOATS.

IN THE SPRING OF 1540, AN EXPEDITION OF 300 SPANIARDS, 800 INDIAN SLAVES, 1,000 HORSES, AND HERDS OF PIGS AND GOATS LEFT MEXICO. THE GOLDEN "SEVEN CITIES OF CIBOLA"—AS THEY WERE CALLED—WAS THEIR OBJECTIVE.

I FOUND THE DESERT WARM..

THEIR LEADER WAS CORONADO, GOVERNOR OF THE MEXICAN FRONTIER, WHO DID HIS EXPLORING IN FULL ARMOR!

DO YOU KNOW ANY MORE CUSS WORDS I CAN CALL DE VACA?

I RAN OUT AFTER THE THIRD "CITY."

THE "SEVEN CITIES" TURNED OUT TO BE THE MUD DWELLINGS OF THE PUEBLO INDIANS IN NEW MEXICO, WHO THREW ROCKS AT THE SPANIARDS. CORONADO LED HIS BAND EASTWARD...

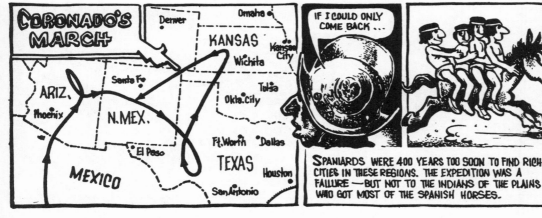

CORONADO'S MARCH

Denver — Omaha
KANSAS
Kansas City
Wichita
ARIZ.
Santa Fe
Tulsa
Phoenix
Okla. City
N. MEX.
Ft. Worth • Dallas
El Paso
TEXAS
Houston
MEXICO
San Antonio

IF I COULD ONLY COME BACK...

SPANIARDS WERE 400 YEARS TOO SOON TO FIND RICH CITIES IN THESE REGIONS. THE EXPEDITION WAS A FAILURE—BUT NOT TO THE INDIANS OF THE PLAINS WHO GOT MOST OF THE SPANISH HORSES.

4,599,999 STEPS... 4,600,000 STEPS... PUFF! PUFF!

HISTORIANS KNOW THE EXPEDITION WENT 2500 MILES, BECAUSE CORONADO ASSIGNED SOLDIERS TO PACE OFF EVERY STEP OF THE WAY FROM MEXICO!

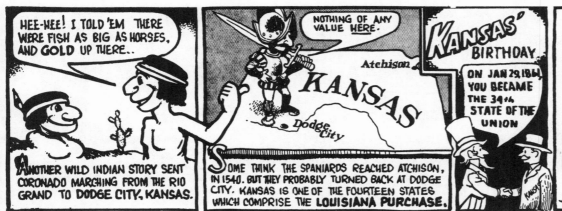

HEE-HEE! I TOLD 'EM THERE WERE FISH AS BIG AS HORSES, AND GOLD UP THERE..

ANOTHER WILD INDIAN STORY SENT CORONADO MARCHING FROM THE RIO GRANDE TO DODGE CITY, KANSAS.

NOTHING OF ANY VALUE HERE.

Atchison
KANSAS
Dodge City

SOME THINK THE SPANIARDS REACHED ATCHISON, IN 1540. BUT THEY PROBABLY TURNED BACK AT DODGE CITY. KANSAS IS ONE OF THE FOURTEEN STATES WHICH COMPRISE THE LOUISIANA PURCHASE.

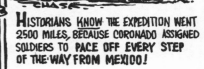

KANSAS' BIRTHDAY

ON JAN 29, 1861 YOU BECAME THE 34th STATE OF THE UNION

NOTHING OF VALUE, CONQUISTADOR? IN 1950, KANSAS FARM INCOME ALONE TOTALED $1,008,140,000.00

GOSH! I SHOULD OF STUCK AROUND 410 YEARS!

AFTER THE DISASTERS OF DESOTO AND CORONADO, SPAIN, IN EFFECT, GAVE THE COUNTRY BACK TO THE INDIANS...

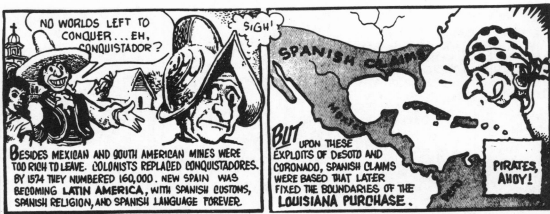

BESIDES MEXICAN AND SOUTH AMERICAN MINES WERE TOO RICH TO LEAVE. COLONISTS REPLACED CONQUISTADORES. BY 1574 THEY NUMBERED 160,000. NEW SPAIN WAS BECOMING **LATIN AMERICA**, WITH SPANISH CUSTOMS, SPANISH RELIGION, AND SPANISH LANGUAGE FOREVER.

BUT UPON THESE EXPLOITS OF DESOTO AND CORONADO, SPANISH CLAIMS WERE BASED THAT LATER FIXED THE BOUNDARIES OF THE **LOUISIANA PURCHASE**.

LIKE FLIES TO HONEY, PIRATES ARE ATTRACTED TO TREASURE. AT THE TIME OF THE LOUISIANA PURCHASE RIVER PIRATES PREYED ON THE RICH COMMERCE OF THE MISSISSIPPI VALLEY, JUST AS SPAIN WAS HARASSED THREE CENTURIES EARLIER BY THE FIERCE **BUCCANEERS OF THE SPANISH MAIN!**

FRANCE AND ENGLAND, ENVIOUS OF SPAIN, OPENLY BACKED THE BUCCANEERS. MANY OF THEIR ADVENTUROUS SONS ADOPTED PIRACY CAREERS AGAINST SPAIN AS THEIR "PATRIOTIC" DUTY..

ALSO THE PAY IS VERY GOOD!

BUT DIFFERENT FROM MOST WAS THE FRENCHMAN, SAMUEL CHAMPLAIN. HE VISITED THE SPANISH MAINLAND, SPIED ALL AROUND, AND WROTE A BOOK WHICH IMPRESSED THE KING OF FRANCE.

1534 - 1543

WHILE DESOTO WAS DISCOVERING A RIVER NEAR MEMPHIS, CORONADO WAS TOURING KANSAS, AND CARTIER WAS EXPLORING ANOTHER RIVER — THE ONE HE NAMED "ST. LAWRENCE".

TOURIST SEASON — UGH!

60 YEARS LATER.. A DUTCH AND A FRENCH SHIP SAILED FOR NORTH AMERICA. UNKNOWN TO EACH OTHER, EACH WAS SEEKING THAT **NORTHWEST PASSAGE** TO CHINA.

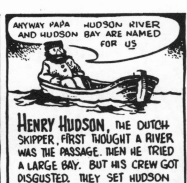

HENRY HUDSON, THE DUTCH SKIPPER, FIRST THOUGHT A RIVER WAS THE PASSAGE. THEN HE TRIED A LARGE BAY. BUT HIS CREW GOT DISGUSTED. THEY SET HUDSON AND HIS LITTLE BOY ADRIFT IN A SKIFF, AND SAILED HOME.

BUT THE FRENCH SHIP BROUGHT SAMUEL DE CHAMPLAIN

WATCH ME TOMORROW.

CHAMPLAIN HAD MINGLED WITH THE MONEY-MAD SPANIARDS, BUT HE NEVER GOT THEIR LUST FOR GOLD. CHAMPLAIN WAS HUNGRY FOR INFORMATION....

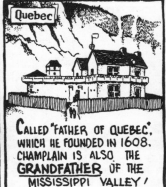

CALLED "FATHER OF QUEBEC", WHICH HE FOUNDED IN 1608. CHAMPLAIN IS ALSO THE **GRANDFATHER** OF THE MISSISSIPPI VALLEY!

UNABLE TO GO EVERYWHERE HIMSELF, HE SENT MANY YOUNG FRENCHMEN OUT EXPLORING...THUS HE SET THE PATTERN OF NORTH AMERICAN EXPLORATION. HE HAD CREATED THE **COUREURS DE BOIS!**

"NICE BEADS...FOR CANOE LOAD OF OL' FURS"

UNLIKE THE SPANIARDS WHO KILLED OR ENSLAVED THE INDIANS, THE FRENCH IN CANADA MADE FRIENDS WITH THEIR INDIAN NEIGHBORS.

"FORTUNATELY, I DON'T UNDERSTAND FRENCH"

ONE NATION OF INDIANS SHAVED THEIR HEADS, EXCEPT FOR A BRISTLE ON TOP. TO THE FRENCH, THIS LOOKED LIKE THE *HURE*, OR BRISTLE ON A PIG'S BACK. SO THEY CALLED THEM **HURONS.**

"YOU OUR FRIEND. SO YOU COME SHOOT GUN AT IROQUOIS"

"TO KEEP THEIR FRIENDSHIP, I'LL HAVE TO GO"

FOR YEARS THESE HURONS HAD BEEN AT WAR WITH SOME OTHER INDIANS, CALLED **IROQUOIS.** ONE DAY THEY CAME AND ASKED THE AID OF CHAMPLAIN IN A SCHEDULED BATTLE WITH THEIR ENEMY.

WITH HIS HURON ALLIES, CHAMPLAIN JOURNEYED DOWN THE "RIVER OF THE IROQUOIS" (NOW THE RICHELIEU) INTO BEAUTIFUL LAKE CHAMPLAIN, WHICH IS NAMED AFTER HIM.

"DEATH TO ALL FRENCHMEN!"

NEAR WHERE TICONDEROGA, N.Y. NOW IS THEY MET THE IROQUOIS. CHAMPLAIN ADVANCED TO WITHIN TWENTY FEET AND BLASTED TWO CHIEFS INTO THE HAPPY HUNTING GROUND. THE BATTLE WAS WON.

THUS, IN 1609, BEGAN THE HATE OF ALL IROQUOIS FOR ALL FRENCHMEN. AND, ON THIS VERY DAY, JUST 300 MILES AWAY...

HENRY HUDSON WAS IN THE RIVER NAMED FOR HIM, CLAIMING THESE LANDS FOR THE DUTCH WHO WOULD SUPPLY GUNS TO THE IROQUOIS - AND **TROUBLE FOR THE FRENCH!**

"THAT **MUST** BE THE PACIFIC OCEAN!"

ONE DAY, ONE OF CHAMPLAIN'S COUREURS RETURNED TO REPORT HE HAD SEEN A LARGE BODY OF **SALTY** WATER.

"I LIED...IT ISN'T SALTY!"

TO THE DISMAY OF THE COUREUR, CHAMPLAIN DECIDED TO VISIT THIS "SALTY" SEA HIMSELF.

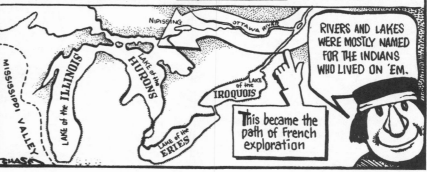

UP THE RIVER OF THE OTTAWA INDIANS, THROUGH THE LAKE OF THE NIPISSINGS, ONWARD UNTIL JULY 1615, WHEN THE **LAKE OF THE HURONS** WAS DISCOVERED.

RIVERS AND LAKES WERE MOSTLY NAMED FOR THE INDIANS WHO LIVED ON 'EM.

This became the path of French exploration

ON CHRISTMAS DAY IN 1635, CHAMPLAIN DIED. CANADIANS TODAY CONSIDER HIM THE FATHER OF THEIR COUNTRY, NOT OF QUEBEC ALONE.

DURING HIS LIFETIME HIS COUREURS DE BOIS RANGED FAR WESTWARD, TRADING WITH INDIANS, DISCOVERING WONDEROUS NEW LANDS...TO THE VERY FRINGE OF THE MISSISSIPPI VALLEY THEY VENTURED!!

"IROQUOIS TELL ALL INDIANS WHERE THEY GET OFF!"

"...AND IROQUOIS WIVES TELL IROQUOIS YOU SEE. **NEXT WEEK!**"

BUT HE BET WRONG WHEN HE SIDED AGAINST THE IROQUOIS. HE DIDN'T KNOW THESE WERE THE MOST FORMIDABLE OF **ALL** NORTH AMERICAN INDIANS. FRENCHMEN, ALAS, SOON FOUND OUT

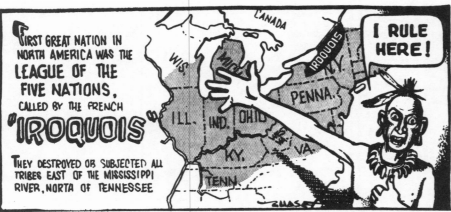

First great nation in North America was the **LEAGUE OF THE FIVE NATIONS,** called by the French **"IROQUOIS"**

They destroyed or subjected all tribes east of the Mississippi River, north of Tennessee

I RULE HERE!

AND I RULE HERE!

Less than 20,000 in number, they lived in 14 villages in what is Northern New York today. (See map.) They lived in long houses, 20 or more family circles per house, and ALL the women were related.   (Iroquois Secret Weapon.)

The Iroquois secret: **UNITY!** Although out-numbered 20 to 1 by other tribes, these five nations were linked in strong social, military bonds

MOHAWK · ONONDAGO · CAYUGA · ONEIDA · SENECA

WOMAN WAS SUPREME! — Inheritance was through the mother's line, never the father's

All property, political offices, **EVERYTHING** belonged to the woman and **HER** family

HELLO MOTHERS!

All of one tribe, or family, were considered brothers and sisters. There could be hundreds. A bride brought her husband (always of another family or tribe) to live with **her** mother's tribe. And her mother—plus all of **her** sisters— all became his **MOTHERS-IN-LAW!**

One historian believes this is what made the Iroquois so **WARLIKE!**

ALL I WANT IS **PEACE!**

The Iroquois spent most of their history at war against tribes who broke the peace, or whom they thought might break it. Later, an economic factor stimulated their aggression ..

THIS WAS THE FUR TRADE. Englishmen traded with their allies, the Iroquois. Frenchmen did business with **ALL** the other anti-Iroquois Indians.

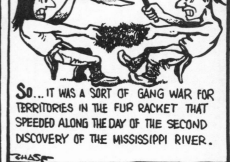

So... it was a sort of gang war for territories in the fur racket that speeded along the day of the second discovery of the Mississippi River.

BEADS FOR BEARSKINS?

The **COUREURS DE BOIS,** whom Champlain recruited in the interests of geography and exploration, soon settled down to the business of trading for **FURS**

Further and further west they went, ever seeking the "unspoiled" Indian, who would trade a fortune in furs for a trinket or two

No path finders these but **PATHMAKERS!** Others would follow, and become famous names in history books ... But the coureurs de bois were just **BUSINESS MEN** —

BESIDES THE COUREUR DE BOIS **MISSIONARIES** MADE IMPORTANT CONTRIBUTIONS TO NORTH AMERICAN EXPLORATION TO SAVE SOULS. THE FATHERS WENT *EVERYWHERE!*

MISSIONARY MARQUETTE SHARES EQUAL HONOR WITH JOLIET, THE COUREUR, FOR THE DISCOVERY OF THE MISSISSIPPI —

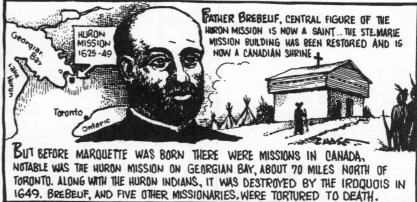

FATHER BREBEUF, CENTRAL FIGURE OF THE HURON MISSION IS NOW A SAINT.. THE STE. MARIE MISSION BUILDING HAS BEEN RESTORED AND IS NOW A CANADIAN SHRINE

BUT BEFORE MARQUETTE WAS BORN THERE WERE MISSIONS IN CANADA. NOTABLE WAS THE HURON MISSION ON GEORGIAN BAY, ABOUT 70 MILES NORTH OF TORONTO. ALONG WITH THE HURON INDIANS, IT WAS DESTROYED BY THE IROQUOIS IN 1649. BREBEUF, AND FIVE OTHER MISSIONARIES, WERE TORTURED TO DEATH.

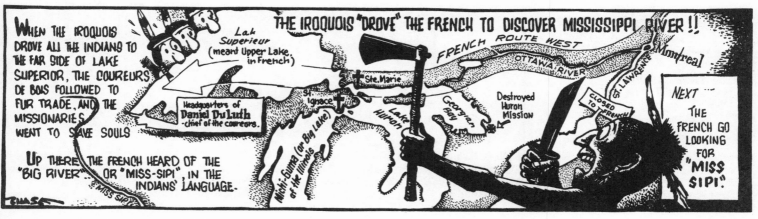

THE IROQUOIS "DROVE" THE FRENCH TO DISCOVER MISSISSIPPI RIVER!!

WHEN THE IROQUOIS DROVE ALL THE INDIANS TO THE FAR SIDE OF LAKE SUPERIOR, THE COUREURS DE BOIS FOLLOWED TO FUR TRADE, AND THE MISSIONARIES WENT TO SAVE SOULS

UP THERE THE FRENCH HEARD OF THE "BIG RIVER" OR "MISS-SIPI", IN THE INDIANS' LANGUAGE.

NEXT -- THE FRENCH GO LOOKING FOR "MISS SIPI".

WHEN CHAMPLAIN DIED, CANADA ALMOST DIED TOO, MURDEROUSLY, AT THE HANDS OF THE IROQUOIS INDIANS.

THEN.. THE MAN FOR WHOM LOUISIANA IS NAMED SAVED CANADA! — LOUIS XIV MADE IT A ROYAL PROVINCE. PREVIOUSLY, CANADA HAD BEEN RENTED OUT TO "PROPRIETORS" WHO WERE SUPPOSED TO COLONIZE IT IN RETURN FOR ALL THE FUR PROFITS.

YOU'RE WELCOME GOVERNOR — ESPECIALLY YOUR REGIMENT

ABLE MEN WERE SENT TO ADMINISTER THE COLONY'S AFFAIRS... AND A WHOLE REGIMENT TO FIGHT THE IROQUOIS.

FIND OUT WHERE THAT RIVER *GOES!*

THE NEW GOVERNOR, FRONTENAC, LOST NO TIME RESUMING WESTWARD EXPLORATION. LOUIS JOLLIET, AN EXPERIENCED COUREUR DE BOIS, WAS ORDERED TO GO FIND THAT RIVER CALLED, "MISS SIPI".

A PRAYER OF MINE HAS BEEN ANSWERED.

AS WAS THE FRENCH CUSTOM, A MISSIONARY WOULD GO ALONG. FATHER JACQUES MARQUETTE RECEIVED THE ASSIGNMENT.

THIS DAY WE LEAVE ST. IGNACE MISSION.

FIVE OTHER COUREURS JOINED UP. TWO CANOES WERE MADE READY, AND ON MAY 17, 1673 JOLIET AND MARQUETTE SET OUT UPON THEIR JOURNEY THAT WOULD FOREVER LINK THEIR NAMES WITH THE VALLEY OF THE MISSISSIPPI.

IT TOOK MARQUETTE AND JOLIET ONLY..

MAY 17__DEPARTURE FROM ST. IGNACE.
JUNE 1__ENTERED GREEN BAY.
JUNE 17__AT PORTAGE BETWEEN FOX AND WISCONSIN RIVERS.
JUNE 25__MET, VISITED ILLINOIS INDIANS.
JULY 17__ARRIVED, RIVER OF ARKANSAS INDIANS.

61 DAYS!

ALL OF THE NAMES SHOWN ON MAP, NOW SO FAMILIAR, WERE FIRST RECORDED BY MARQUETTE ON THIS TRIP.

THE ILLINOIS RIVER WILL BE SHORTER.. AND THE CHICAGO PORTAGE.

THEY HURRIED BACK TO TELL FRONTENAC. (Death for Marquette, and Disaster for Joliet...)

I'LL EAT IT IF IT KILLS ME!

IN HIS DIARY, FATHER MARQUETTE TELLS HOW HE ALWAYS ATE WITH THE INDIANS HE AND JOLIET MET ON THEIR HISTORIC TRIP. HE WANTED TO SHOW HOW FRIENDLY HE WAS.

INDIAN COOKING DID KILL HIM. WHEREAS, THE HURON MISSIONARIES WERE KILLED BY UNFRIENDLY INDIANS, GENTLE FATHER MARQUETTE WAS MARTYRED BY THE FRIENDLY ONES.

MEANWHILE, JOLIET RACED TO TELL FRONTENAC OF THE TRIP. WITHIN SIGHT OF MONTREAL, HIS CANOE TURNED OVER. HE LOST ALL HIS RECORDS.

AS AN EXPLORER, YOU'RE ALL WET.

SO, JOLIET LOST FAVOR WITH THE GOVERNOR. LASALLE REPLACED HIM.

I'VE GOT A FRIEND NAMED LASALLE.

FRONTENAC... CALLED SAVIOR OF THE CANADA CHAMPLAIN FOUNDED, MADE LOUISIANA POSSIBLE WHEN HE TURNED LASALLE LOOSE IN THE MISSISSIPPI VALLEY.

I'VE GOT PLANS.

LASALLE WILL TRADE THE BEST BEADS FOR YOUR FUR.

LASALLE WAS NO STORY-BOOK HERO, BUT A HARD-HEADED BUSINESSMAN WHO WANTED TO CORNER THE FUR BUSINESS. EVERYTHING HE DID WAS TO THIS END.

IF YOU'RE A GOOD INDIAN, I'LL GET YOU A JOB IN MY SHIPYARD.

OBLIVIOUS TO DANGER AS HE WENT ABOUT HIS BUSINESS AFFAIRS, HE INVADED IROQUOIS COUNTRY, DISCOVERED THE OHIO RIVER, AND BUILT A SHIP ON LAKE ERIE.

I'M HENRI TONTI..

NO MIDWESTERN BUSINESSMAN EVER HAD A RIGHT HAND MAN LIKE LASALLE — THE FIRST BUSINESSMAN IN THE MIDWEST.

CLANG!

BECAUSE TONTI'S RIGHT HAND WAS IRON, REPLACING THE ONE HE LOST IN BATTLE. TROUBLESOME INDIANS CAME TO RESPECT THIS RIGHT HAND OF LASALLE'S RIGHT HAND MAN...

Peoria, Illinois In 1680

TONTI WAS IRONLIKE IN MANY WAYS... HE HAD FAITH IN LASALLE, AND HE MAINTAINED THE TRADING OUTPOSTS BUILT ON THE ILLINOIS FRONTIER BY LASALLE.

IF WE COULD EXPORT FURS DOWN THE MISSISSIPPI, WE WOULD ELUDE THE IROQUOIS. GOOD IDEA, LASALLE

BUT- THE IROQUOIS, FUR-HUNTING FOR THE ENGLISH, INVADED ILLINOIS. ONCE MORE THE IROQUOIS PUSH ALONG FRENCH EXPLORATION — THIS TIME TO THE MOUTH OF THE MISSISSIPPI!

LOUISIANA PURCHASE

LaSalle was the first businessman to buy influence with furs! That was the way he stayed in Frontenac's favor, and he got the permission of King Louis XIV to go discover Louisiana by presenting HIM with a fur coat.

LaSalle was always broke. Instead of salary, he gave Tonti an interest in his fur business. Then, he had to borrow money from Tonti to finance his historic trip. The King wouldn't pay expenses.

Although careless in money matters, LaSalle was a thorough planner. Near Peoria, he starting building a ship—a warship—for the expedition to the mouth of the Mississippi.

Raiding Iroquois prevented completion of his ship. LaSalle used canoes for his expedition. His force numbered 54. Included were 23 coureurs de bois; 18 Indians, 10 of whom insisted on bringing their squaws—and 3 had children.

On Jan. 4, 1683 the expedition was at Chicago. It was midwinter. Canoes had to be dragged over snow as far as Peoria, where the river was free of ice.

Father Membre, who went along, kept a record. He reported southern Indians more polite and hospitable.

...And Tonti also made the trip.

LaSalle's trip took twice as long as Marquette and Joliet's. But on April 9, 1682 he reached the Mississippi's mouth.

Never before nor since have the swamps at Southwest Pass witnessed an affair like LaSalle's ceremony of taking possession. A cross was raised, songs were sung, and LaSalle read his proclamation, which was both long and legal. Also, an official lead plaque was buried in the mud.

A few years ago a fisherman found LaSalle's lead plaque, with the seal of France on it. But before excited historians could reach his remote shack, he had chopped it up to weight down his shrimp nets.

LaSalle's Louisiana..

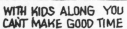
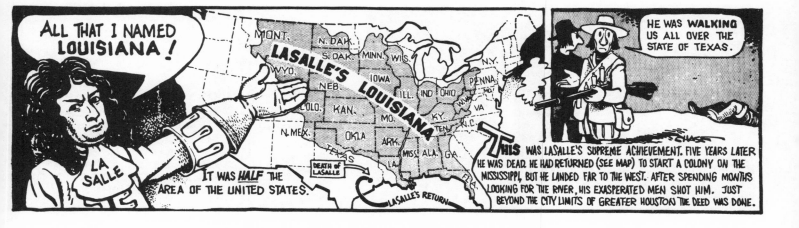

All that I named Louisiana! It was HALF the area of the United States.

He was walking us all over the state of Texas.

This was LaSalle's supreme achievement. Five years later he was dead. He had returned (see map) to start a colony on the Mississippi, but he landed far to the west. After spending months looking for the river, his exasperated men shot him. Just beyond the city limits of greater Houston the deed was done.

IT WAS WITH ALL THE LEGALITY OF AN ACT OF SALE THAT LASALLE TRANSFERRED LOUISIANA FROM THE INDIANS TO FRANCE. HE DESCRIBED THE PROPERTY AS ALL LANDS DRAINED BY THE MISSISSIPPI — PLUS ALL THE GULF COAST EASTWARD TO THE FIRST SPANISH CLAIM OF RECORD, WHICH WAS SOUTH OF SARASOTA, FLA.

NONE COULD CHALLENGE LASALLE'S CLAIM. IT WAS ALL ACCORDING TO LAW, BUT TEN YEARS AFTER HIS DEATH, SPAIN AND ENGLAND GOT A NEW LAW PASSED!

TO SECURE FRENCH OWNERSHIP OF LOUISIANA, LOUIS XIV HUSTLED OFF **IBERVILLE**, A FAMOUS CANADIAN HERO, TO ESTABLISH A SETTLEMENT AT THE GULF END OF THE MISSISSIPPI RIVER.

IBERVILLE ESTABLISHED FORTS AT BILOXI AND MOBILE. TONTI JOINED HIM. HIS FUR BUSINESS IN ILLINOIS GREW SO PROSPEROUS THAT THE GOVERNMENT DECIDED TO TAKE IT.

BUT, ALAS — BOTH IBERVILLE AND TONTI DIED IN A YELLOW FEVER EPIDEMIC. ALSO, FRANCE GOT BUSY IN EUROPEAN WARS. LOUISIANA WAS FORGOTTEN, AND ALMOST DIED TOO.

SAVIOR OF LOUISIANA, AS CHAMPLAIN HAD BEEN OF CANADA, WAS **BIENVILLE** — KID BROTHER OF IBERVILLE. SOMEHOW, FOR TEN YEARS HE KEPT THINGS GOING. THEN — IN 1716 — THE KING DIED... AND HE LEFT FRANCE BANKRUPT.

WHEN IBERVILLE AND BIENVILLE WERE FOUNDING FRENCH SETTLEMENTS ON THE GULFCOAST OF LOUISIANA, OTHER COUREURS DE BOIS WERE PADDLING UP THE MISSOURI RIVER. NOTABLE OF THESE EARLY EXPLORERS OF THE WESTERN REACHES OF FRENCH LOUISIANA WERE **THE MALLETS**.

INDIANS DIRECTED THESE TWO MALLET BROTHERS TO A RIVER THEY CALLED "NI-BTHASKA". OVERLAND, FROM ITS SOURCE, THEY REACHED SANTA FE. AND - BY ANOTHER RIVER NOW NAMED "CANADIAN" FOR THESE TWO CANADIAN BROTHERS - THEY RETURNED TO NEW ORLEANS.

NEBRASKA'S Birthday On March 1, 1867, Nebraska became the 37th State of the UNION.

NI-BTHASKA, OR NEBRASKA, MEANS "RIVER SPREAD OUT FLAT". THE MALLETS CHANGED IT INTO A FRENCH WORD FOR FLAT OR PLATE-LIKE. THEY NAMED IT **PLATTE**.

WHEN LOUIS XIV DIED, HIS HEIR — LOUIS XV — WAS JUST A BABY. SO THE DUKE OF ORLEANS RULED AS REGENT. THINGS WEREN'T SO EASY FOR THE DUKE, BECAUSE FRANCE WAS SPENDING ABOUT $13,000,000 A YEAR MORE THAN IT WAS TAKING IN...

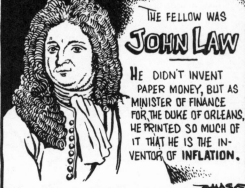

THE FELLOW WAS **JOHN LAW** HE DIDN'T INVENT PAPER MONEY, BUT AS MINISTER OF FINANCE FOR THE DUKE OF ORLEANS, HE PRINTED SO MUCH OF IT THAT HE IS THE INVENTOR OF **INFLATION**.

LAW'S PAPER MONEY WAS FIRST SECURED BY THE REVENUE OF FRANCE. THEN, TO BACK UP **MORE** PAPER MONEY, HE UNDERTOOK TO COLONIZE AND EXPLOIT THE "RICHES" OF **LOUISIANA**.

FIRST ADVERTISER OF LOUISIANA WAS FATHER HENNEPIN. HE WAS ONE OF FOUR PRIESTS ASSIGNED TO LASALLE'S VENTURES. IN 1680, LASALLE SENT TWO COUREURS DE BOIS TO EXPLORE THE SOURCE OF THE MISSISSIPPI, AND FATHER HENNEPIN ACCOMPANIED THEM.

HIS BOOK BECAME A BEST SELLER IN EUROPE. SOME SAY THE AUTHOR EXAGGERATED, AND THAT HE GAVE HIMSELF TOO MUCH CREDIT — ESPECIALLY, IN A LATER EDITION, WHEN HE ADDED THAT **HE** DISCOVERED THE RIVER'S MOUTH, AND NOT LASALLE.

TIME HAS PROVEN THAT FATHER HENNEPIN DID NOT EXAGGERATE THE RICHNESS OF LOUISIANA... AND 235 YEARS AGO HE INFLUENCED JOHN LAW, WHO SUPPLIED THE COLONY'S GREATEST NEED — **PEOPLE.**

ALTHOUGH IN POWER ONLY FIVE YEARS, JOHN LAW ACCOMPLISHED MUCH - BOTH FOR GOOD AND EVIL. HE INCREASED THE POPULATION OF LOUISIANA FROM 700 TO ABOUT 8000, AND THAT WAS GOOD.

PROMOTION OF HIS MISSISSIPPI COMPANY STOCK DETERMINED ALL LAW'S ACTIONS. BESIDES AN IMPRESSIVE NUMBER OF COLONISTS, HE HAD TO HAVE A CITY **ON** THE RIVER. LAW PLANNED IT HIMSELF.

BIENVILLE BECAME GOVERNOR AGAIN. A PREVIOUS "PROPRIETOR OF LOUISIANA" HAD REPLACED HIM WITH **LAMOTHE CADILLAC**, WHO FOUNDED DETROIT. NOW BIENVILLE HAD ORDERS TO FOUND ANOTHER CITY, AND **HIS** REASON FOR NEW ORLEANS WAS THE SAME AS CADILLAC'S FOR DETROIT...

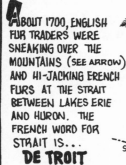

ABOUT 1700, ENGLISH FUR TRADERS WERE SNEAKING OVER THE MOUNTAINS (SEE ARROW) AND HI-JACKING FRENCH FURS AT THE STRAIT BETWEEN LAKES ERIE AND HURON. THE FRENCH WORD FOR STRAIT IS... **DE TROIT**

TO STOP THIS, LAMOTHE CADILLAC AND 100 MEN WERE RUSHED TO DETROIT TO BUILD A FORT.

AT THIS SAME TIME, BIENVILLE (THEN A TEEN-AGER) MET AN ENGLISH SHIP SAILING UP THE MISSISSIPPI. TELLING THEM A FRENCH FORT WAS JUST AHEAD, HE FOOLED THE ENGLISH INTO TURNING BACK. THIS BEND IN THE RIVER - 20 MILES BELOW NEW ORLEANS - IS STILL CALLED "ENGLISH TURN."

BIENVILLE WAITED ON THE BEACHES OF BILOXI EIGHTEEN YEARS BEFORE HE WAS PERMITTED TO FOUND NEW ORLEANS, THE PORT CITY THAT WOULD MAKE THE LOUISIANA PURCHASE NECESSARY IN 85 YEARS.

HOW SO FEW FRENCHMEN, WITH SO FEW SETTLEMENTS HELD ON TO THE VAST LOUISIANA REGION AS LONG AS THEY DID AMAZES ALL HISTORIANS.

BUT TIME FOR THE FRENCH IN NORTH AMERICA WAS RUNNING OUT. ENGLISH COLONISTS WERE PEEKING OVER THE APPALACHIANS... THE MISSISSIPPI RIVER VALLEY - LASALLE'S LOUISIANA - LOOKED MIGHTY GOOD TO THEM ... AND THEY OUT-NUMBERED THE FRENCH OWNERS 20 TO 1!

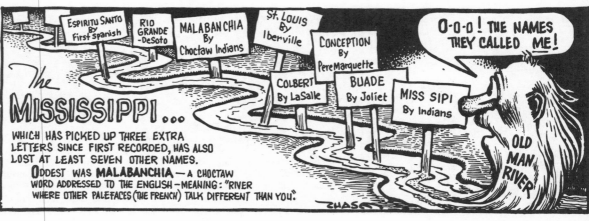

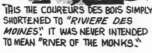

As early as Marquette and Joliet, English fur traders were crossing the mountains, and ranging as far west as the Mississippi. Fur was the best money crop in the English colonies.

But different than these were the LONG HUNTERS, so called for the sometimes year long hunts made in the wilderness of Louisiana.

Back home in a frontier cabin in a clearing, his family awaited the return of this early model of the "American small business man".

The governor of Canada—alarmed at the boldness of English long hunters and traders—sent out an expedition to bury lead plaques along the Ohio River. These plaques proclaimed French ownership.

Also the French built two forts at the portage between Lake Erie and the Allegheny River. This alarmed the Governor of Virginia.

So in midwinter of 1753, a 21-year old major of the Virginia Militia was sent to tell the French to get out. George Washington was this major.

With outstretched arms the Ohio River Valley seemed to beckon to many new immigrants to the English colonies in the early 1700's.

This is why—in 1747—the Ohio Company was organized. The company planned a "suburb" beyond the mountains in the wilderness of LaSalle's Louisiana.

So—besides poaching traders and long hunters, the Ohio Company angered the French.

Early Ohio Company grants included most of the present-day state of West Virginia.

On April 16, 1754, a strong French force surprised Ohio Co. workmen building a fort at the forks of the Ohio. This was the beginning of the FRENCH AND INDIAN WAR...

The French and their Indians won at first. The more numerous English, in several colonies, weren't organized. Benjamin Franklin printed this famous cartoon urging unity.

The Indians' Dilemma...

OHIO INDIANS PREFERRED TO TRADE WITH THE ENGLISH. THEIR GOODS WERE BETTER AND CHEAPER, BUT THE ENGLISH CLEARED THE LAND AND BUILT CABINS — SO THE INDIANS SIDED WITH THE FRENCH.

...AND AS LONG AS THEY HAD PRESENTS FOR THE INDIANS, THEY HAD INDIAN ALLIES.

THE ENGLISH BLOCKADE OF THE SEA LANES LOST THE WAR IN THE OHIO VALLEY FOR THE FRENCH. THEY LOST ALL CANADA, AND LOUISIANA TOO.

PITTSBURGH WAS NAMED FOR **WILLIAM PITT** — HIS STATESMANSHIP WON THE WAR AGAINST FRANCE, — BUT THEN HE LOST HIS JOB, AND ON ACCOUNT OF LOUISIANA — SEE TOMORROW.

PRIME MINISTER PITT WANTED TO GO TO WAR ALL OVER AGAIN, WHEN FRANCE AND SPAIN MADE A SECRET DEAL WHEREBY FRANCE GAVE SPAIN HALF OF LASALLE'S LOUISIANA, INCLUDING NEW ORLEANS.

BUT THE BRITISH LION HAD BITTEN OFF MORE THAN HE COULD CHEW — EVEN WITH HALF OF LOUISIANA.

WHEN ENGLAND SUGGESTED THAT THE AMERICANS HELP PAY THE COSTS OF CONQUERING ALL OF EASTERN LOUISIANA, TROUBLE STARTED.

NEW AT WORLD LEADERSHIP IN THE 1760'S, JOHN BULL HAD HIS HANDS FULL TRYING TO PROTECT THE SETTLERS FROM THE INDIANS, AND THE INDIANS FROM THE SETTLERS.

ALSO, AMERICAN COLONISTS WEREN'T TOO HAPPY ABOUT HAVING TO SUPPORT BRITISH TROOPS. . . .

MEANWHILE, SPECULATORS BEGAN BUYING LAND FROM THE INDIANS TO ESTABLISH COLONIES IN LOUISIANA.

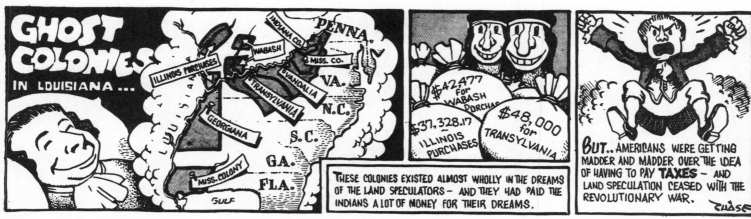

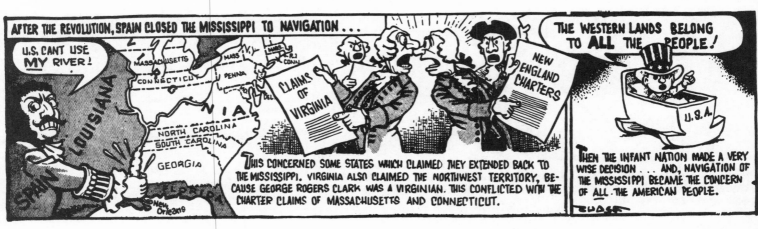

THE CONESTOGA WAGONS BROUGHT BETTER ROADS. BUT THE NEW NATION WAS BROKE, AND EARLY ROADS WERE FINANCED BY TOLLS. A SPIKED, OR PIKED, TOLL GATE WAS OPENED UPON PAYMENT.

HERE'S MY 14¢. TURN YOUR PIKE!

BUT, MOST IMPORTANT, THOSE WAGONS KEPT FRONTIER SETTLERS IN TOUCH WITH THE HOME GOVERNMENT.

EVER SINCE CONESTOGA WAGON DAYS, U.S. TOLL ROADS HAVE BEEN CALLED TURNPIKES... ALSO, BECAUSE THESE DRIVERS RODE THE LEFT REAR HORSE, THEY PASSED ONCOMING TRAFFIC ON THE RIGHT SO THEY COULD SEE. IN THE U.S., TRAFFIC STILL KEEPS TO THE RIGHT.

HOW'D YOU ENJOY THE TRIP?

OH, PRETTY GOOD — FOR A HORSE.

CONESTOGA WAGON HORSES WERE A SPECIAL BREED, AND THE DRIVERS WERE SOMETHING SPECIAL TOO. OLD TIMERS INSIST THESE TWO USED TO TALK TO EACH OTHER!..

THEY'RE SIX FOR 5¢, THESE CONESTOGA SPECIALS — WE CALL 'EM "STOGIES", FOR SHORT.

BESIDES "TURNPIKE" AND "DRIVE TO RIGHT", THESE WAGONERS ALSO LEFT US A NAME FOR A CHEAP CIGAR.

Menu
Ham & Eggs, Beefsteak, Fried Speckled Trout Fried Potatoes, Griddlecakes, Preserves, Pickles, Pie, Cheese, Cake, Coffee
Price 12¢ (NO TAX)

YEAH, BUT I GOTTA TIP 10%.

BUT...

REGULAR HIGHWAY TRAFFIC, INITIATED BY CONESTOGA WAGONS, WAS SOON ACCOMMODATED BY ROADSIDE INNS. THIS IS ACTUAL MENU OF AN INN NEAR PITTSBURGH.

DANIEL BOONE HAD NO WAGONS ON THE WILDERNESS ROAD

70,000 SETTLERS GOT TO KENTUCKY VIA THE WILDERNESS ROAD. IT WAS THE FIRST ROAD INTO THE OHIO VALLEY. BUT PACK HORSES WERE THE ONLY TRAFFIC THAT COULD USE IT.

Detroit — NORTHWEST TERRITORY — OHIO RIVER — Pittsburgh — Philadelphia — Baltimore — Louisville — Boonesborough — Harrodsburg — KENTUCKY — Ft. Chiswell — Richmond — CUMBERLAND GAP — WILDERNESS ROAD

..AND IT ISN'T EASY FOR ME.

I NEVER GOT PAID FOR IT!

THIS WASN'T MUCH OF A ROAD THAT DANIEL BOONE OPENED UP WITH A TOMAHAWK IN 1775. HOWEVER, DANIEL HAD A COMPLAINT ABOUT THE ROAD TOO.

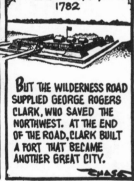

Louisville, Ky. 1782

BUT THE WILDERNESS ROAD SUPPLIED GEORGE ROGERS CLARK, WHO SAVED THE NORTHWEST. AT THE END OF THE ROAD, CLARK BUILT A FORT THAT BECAME ANOTHER GREAT CITY.

HECK!

WHISKEY REBELLION!

...IN PENNSYLVANIA AMERICANS LEARNED THEY HAD TO PAY TAXES.

I'VE GOT THE EQUIVALENT OF 24 SACKS OF RYE ON THIS HORSE.

Next Meet the "Child of the Revolution"

BY 1790, 80,000 LIVED IN SOUTHWESTERN PENNSYLVANIA. MOST WERE FARMERS, BUT A PACKHORSE COULD ONLY CARRY THREE SACKS OF GRAIN TO MARKET, UNLESS IT WAS DISTILLED INTO WHISKEY. SO MOST OF THE FARMERS MADE WHISKEY.

THIS JOB IS FOR THE BIRDS!

TAX BILL

THE U.S. LEVIED AN EXCISE TAX AGAINST THIS FIRST WESTERN INDUSTRY. THE FARMERS REBELLED. TAX COLLECTORS WERE TARRED AND FEATHERED.

YOU CONVINCED ME.

TAXES 2nd Notice

BUT THE U.S. SENT OTHER TAX COLLECTORS, PLUS 13,000 SOLDIERS. EVER SINCE THIS, AMERICAN TAX PAYERS HAVE PAID THEIR TAXES.

SETTLEMENT OF THE OHIO VALLEY HAS BEEN CALLED

CHILD OF THE REVOLUTION...

IN 1775, ABOUT 30,000 LIVED WEST OF THE MOUNTAINS — MOST OF THEM IN KENTUCKY

SO IT WAS THAT THIS "CHILD OF THE REVOLUTION" ESTABLISHED A BEACHHEAD FOR THE GREAT MASS OF SETTLERS, WHEN THEY BEGAN TO COME DOWN THE OHIO RIVER FROM PITTSBURGH.

BEWARE OF INDIANS ON THIS SIDE

LAND SAKES! I SOMETIMES THINK I'D AS SOON HAVE INDIANS IN MY KITCHEN AS YOU COWS

SHOO!

FIRST SETTLERS IN THE KENTUCKY WILDERNESS HAD IT TOUGH. AT FIRST, ALL LIVED IN SMALL STOCKADES, WITH ALL THEIR ANIMALS TOO.

WHEN INDIAN RAIDING SLACKENED, MANY FAMILIES WENT OFF ALONE TO ESTABLISH LAND CLAIMS. THEIR 20 x 30 FOOT CABINS WERE BLEAK AND LONELY PLACES.

HECK, MA — NOTHING TO EAT BUT VENISON AN' WILD TURKEY ..SHUX!

WHATEVER A SETTLER HAD, HE AND HIS WIFE MADE BY HAND. OFTEN, FOR LONG PERIODS, THERE WAS NOTHING TO EAT BUT WILD GAME — HARDLY A BALANCED DIET.

THE KENTUCKY RIFLE

LIKE THE CONESTOGA WAGON, THIS RIFLE WAS PERFECTED IN PENNSYLVANIA.

SECRET OF ITS PERFORMANCE WERE THE OILY PATCHES, KEPT IN HERE. EACH BULLET WAS WRAPPED IN ONE, MAKING A TIGHTER FIT.

OFTEN OVER 5 FEET LONG AND 10 LBS. HEAVY, IT SPUN- OR *RIFLED* - THE BULLET TRUE TO ITS MARK.

DESIGNED FOR HUNTING, IN THE PRACTICED HANDS OF THE AMERICAN FRONTIERSMAN, THIS RIFLE REVOLUTIONIZED WARFARE. IT WON AMERICAN INDEPENDENCE, IT WON THE WILDERNESS ——— IT MADE INEVITABLE THE LOUISIANA PURCHASE.

WOMAN'S WORK ON THE WILDERNESS FRONTIER INCLUDED LOADING RIFLES, TENDING WOUNDED, AND PUTTING OUT HOUSES SET ON FIRE ...

WHEN I GET TIME I MUST GO HOE MY CORN ..

THE FRONTIER MURDERED 'EM.

1st. wife   2nd. wife   3rd. wife

WHEN THERE WAS NO INDIAN TROUBLE, SHE HAD MORE LEISURELY HOUSEHOLD DUTIES...THAT IS, MORE LEISURELY THAN FIGHTING INDIANS.

FRONTIER LIFE WAS ESPECIALLY CRUEL TO WOMEN. MANY A FAMILY BURIAL PLOT GRIMLY SUMS UP THE HEROIC, SELF-SACRIFICING ROLE WOMEN PLAYED.

LOUISIANA PURCHASE

FRONTIER CHILDHOOD
THERE WASN'T MUCH TIME FOR PLAY. SMALL BOYS AND GIRLS DID MANY OF THE CHORES TOGETHER.

BUT ONLY THE GIRLS SPUN, AND KNIT, AND WOVE. THEY BECAME EXPERT AT AN EARLY AGE.

BOYS SPENT LONG HOURS PRACTICING WITH BOW AND ARROW, THE RIFLE, AND THE TOMAHAWK.

WHEN 14, THE BOY WAS GIVEN A RIFLE, AND A MAN'S RESPONSIBILITIES. AND THE GIRL WAS GIVEN IN MARRIAGE.

AS MUCH AS ANYTHING, THE ORDEAL OF THE FIRST SETTLERS IN THE OHIO VALLEY WERE THE BIRTH PANGS OF THE **AMERICAN SPIRIT**... THESE PEOPLE FOUND STRENGTH WITHIN THEMSELVES, COURAGE TO WORK OR FIGHT FOR WHAT THEY HAD WON... THESE PEOPLE DEMANDED THE LOUISIANA PURCHASE!

LATER ARRIVALS TO KENTUCKY, WHO WERE NOT FRONTIER FOLK, ADMIRED THE HEROIC FIRST SETTLERS, AND SOON ACQUIRED THEIR SPIRIT TOO.

BOATS FROM PITTSBURGH COULD GO NO FURTHER DOWN THAN LOUISVILLE, BECAUSE OF DANGEROUS FALLS IN THE RIVER THERE. THAT'S WHY KENTUCKY WAS SETTLED FIRST.

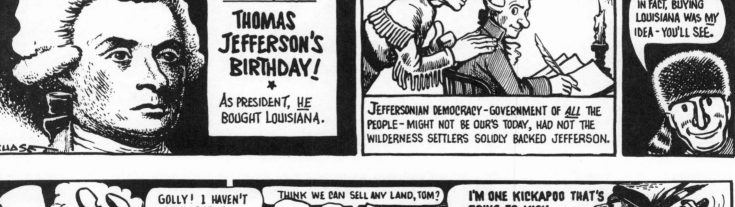

APRIL 13, 1743
THOMAS JEFFERSON'S BIRTHDAY! AS PRESIDENT, HE BOUGHT LOUISIANA.

JEFFERSONIAN DEMOCRACY - GOVERNMENT OF ALL THE PEOPLE - MIGHT NOT BE OUR'S TODAY, HAD NOT THE WILDERNESS SETTLERS SOLIDLY BACKED JEFFERSON.

THE YOUNG UNITED STATES WAS LITERALLY BOWLED OVER BY THE RUSH OF SETTLERS INTO THE OHIO VALLEY SOON AFTER THE REVOLUTIONARY WAR.

SOON CHOICEST KENTUCKY LANDS WERE SETTLED. IN CONGRESS, THOMAS JEFFERSON HEADED A COMMITTEE THAT DREW UP THE FAMOUS "ORDINANCE OF 1787."

BUT... SUCH TRIBES AS THE SHAWNEES, MIAMIS, DELEWARES, AND KICKAPOOS LIVED IN THE NORTHWEST TERRITORY. THEY RESENTED SETTLEMENT OF THEIR HUNTING GROUNDS.

THE ORDINANCE OF 1787 DIVIDED THE NORTHWEST INTO FIVE TERRITORIES. WHEN ANY TERRITORY GOT 60,000 SETTLERS, IT COULD BECOME A **STATE**!

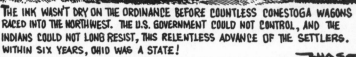

THE INK WASN'T DRY ON THE ORDINANCE BEFORE COUNTLESS CONESTOGA WAGONS RACED INTO THE NORTHWEST. THE U.S. GOVERNMENT COULD NOT CONTROL, AND THE INDIANS COULD NOT LONG RESIST, THIS RELENTLESS ADVANCE OF THE SETTLERS. WITHIN SIX YEARS, OHIO WAS A STATE!

SAY! DOESN'T THIS ENTITLE ME TO A REFUND OF ALL THAT TAX MONEY?

OHIO QUALIFIED FOR STATEHOOD SO QUICKLY THAT CONGRESS <u>NEVER</u> <u>DID</u> OK ONE OF THE PAPERS — THE IMPORTANT ONE WHEREIN OHIO FORMALLY APPLIED FOR STATEHOOD!

I'M A YALE MAN - WHO ARE <u>YOU</u>?

?

DIFFERENT FROM THE FIRST SETTLERS OF KENTUCKY, WERE THOSE WHO SETTLED OHIO AFTER 1787. MANY WERE FROM NEW ENGLAND, AND A LOT OF THEM — LIKE MOSES **CLEVELAND** - WERE COLLEGE GRADUATES!

WE FARED BETTER IN THE AMERICAN REVOLUTION, THAN IN THE FRENCH, EH MARIE?

YEAH - WE LOST OUR HEADS OVER <u>THAT</u> ONE.

RUFUS PUTNAM, ANOTHER NEW ENGLANDER, FOUNDED MARIETTA; NAMED IN HONOR OF MARIE ANTOINETTE, WHO AIDED DURING THE REVOLUTION. (LOUISVILLE, KY. HONORS HER HUSBAND, LOUIS XVI.)

Cincinnati... in 1788.

MANY OF THESE YALE AND HARVARD MEN WERE ALSO ARMY OFFICERS AND FRATERNITY BROTHERS IN THE SOCIETY OF THE **CINCINNATI** — AND THAT'S WHERE ANOTHER OHIO CITY GOT ITS NAME.

GOSH! I SHOULD GO FLY MY KITE!!

BENJAMIN FRANKLIN WAS ONE OF THE THREE DIPLOMATS WHO WON THE MISSISSIPPI AS THE WESTERN BOUNDARY OF THE U.S. FRANKLIN REMARKED, HOWEVER, THAT SETTLEMENT SO FAR WEST WOULDN'T COME FOR A <u>CENTURY OR SO</u>!

WE BOTH HAVE THE SAME BIRTHDAY... JUNE 1!

STATE OF KY

STATE OF TENN.

BUT NINE YEARS AFTER THE TREATY OF PARIS, KENTUCKY WAS A STATE — AND IN FOUR MORE YEARS TENNESSEE WAS A STATE ALSO. (TENNESSEE ALMOST GOT NAMED "FRANKLIN!")

SPAIN

EVEN BEFORE OHIO WAS ADMITTED, MORE THAN 250,000 PEOPLE LIVED IN KENTUCKY, TENNESSEE, AND OHIO. FREE NAVIGATION OF THE MISSISSIPPI RIVER WAS A PROBLEM ALREADY <u>DEMANDING</u> SOLUTION.

IT'S AS MUCH OUR RIVER AS SPAIN'S - WE OWN ONE SIDE!

TEN YEARS AFTER THE REVOLUTION, OHIO RIVER SETTLERS WERE TELLING THE FEDERAL GOVERNMENT TO GET THEM FREE NAVIGATION OF THE MISSISSIPPI — OR THEY WOULD START <u>ANOTHER REVOLUTION</u>.

I HOPE NAPOLEON DOESN'T SEE THIS!

PITTSBURGH GAZETTE
MARCH 3, 1803

THEY EVEN PROVED WITH FIGURES THAT UNCLE SAM COULDN'T AFFORD <u>NOT</u> TO BUY LOUISIANA. ALSO, THEY APPRAISED ITS VALUE MANY TIMES <u>MORE</u> THAN WHAT WAS LATER PAID FOR IT!

THAT'S FOR ME!

WANTED KEELBOAT MEN
FIGHT RIVER PIRATES. SEE SPANIARDS. THE RIVER IS THE NEXT FRONTIER.

MEANWHILE, OUT-OF-WORK INDIAN FIGHTERS WERE BECOMING KEELBOAT MEN, AND DESCENDING ON SPANISH NEW ORLEANS. WATCH 'EM, NEXT WEEK!

Miles OF BOATABLE WATERS IN LaSALLE'S LOUISIANA ARE MORE THAN TWO TIMES AROUND THE EARTH!

THE STORY OF THE MISSISSIPPI VALLEY—OF THE LOUISIANA PURCHASE—IS ALSO A STORY OF **BOATS**. INDIANS DEVELOPED THE GRACEFUL BARK CANOE, AND THE RUGGED DUG-OUT. BOTH OF THESE WERE THE BOATS OF THE EXPLORERS.

I'M NOT PROUD OF THIS ONE...

ANOTHER INDIAN INVENTION WAS THE CRUDE **BULL BOAT**. UNTIL THE TIME OF THE OHIO SETTLERS *THESE* WERE THE ONLY BOATS IN GENERAL USE ON THE 50,000 MILES OF LOUISIANA'S WATERS.

FIRST OTHER THAN INDIAN BOAT USED IN THE MISSISSIPPI VALLEY WAS CALLED **BATEAU**.

BUILT OF PLANKS AND FLAT BOTTOMED, BATEAUX RANGED FROM SKIFF-SIZE UP TO 70 TON CARRIERS.

UGH!

OF COURSE I NEVER BUILT NO BOAT BEFORE THIS.

YOU'RE TELLING ME!

HOW DO WE GO *AGAINST* THE CURRENT?

WE GET OFF AND WALK.

MOVED BY SAILS, OR OARS, OR BOTH, THE BATEAU WAS THE IMPORTANT CRAFT ON THE OHIO FROM THE FRENCH AND INDIAN WAR TO THE REVOLUTION. BUT THE BATEAU WASN'T MUCH OF A BOAT. THE **RAFT** WAS ALMOST AN IMPROVEMENT.

HOW FAST WILL SHE GO?

OH...AT FULL SPEED AHEAD I CAN GO AS FAST AS THE RIVER CAN.

THE MISTAKE OF THE BATEAU BUILDER WAS THAT HE TRIED TO BUILD SOMETHING THAT *LOOKED* LIKE A BOAT. THE **RAFT** DIDN'T LOOK LIKE ANYTHING, BUT IT PROVIDED SIMILAR DOWNSTREAM TRANSPORTATION.

WE'LL JES FLOAT ALONG 'TIL WE FIND SOMETHING BETTER THAN WHAT WE GOT HERE.

RAFTS WERE FAVORITES OF IMMIGRANT FAMILIES. SOME RAFTS WERE AN ACRE LARGE, COMPLETE WITH LOG CABIN AND HAYSTACK, AND LOOKED FOR ALL THE WORLD LIKE BARNYARDS AFLOAT.

NO RAFT FOR US.

WE'RE HIGH CLASS.

MORE DISCRIMINATING IMMIGRANT FAMILIES ACQUIRED **FLATBOATS**. SOME WERE LITTLE MORE THAN RAFTS WITH SIDES. OTHERS WERE REAL FANCY.

MIND MY LACE CURTAINS NOW, LUM.

BETTER CLASS FAMILY FLATBOATS HAD BRICK FIRE-PLACES, AND MANY CONVENIENCES. SOME WERE SAID TO BOAST LACE CURTAINS ON WINDOWS.

WONDER IF THE SPANIARDS WILL LET US UNLOAD AT NEW ORLEANS THIS TIME?

WE NEVER KNOW 'TIL WE GET THERE.

DIFFERENT FROM THE OHIO FAMILY BOAT THAT BROUGHT SETTLERS, WERE THE MISSISSIPPI FLATS THAT BROUGHT OHIO VALLEY PRODUCE TO THE NEW ORLEANS MARKET. USUALLY, FARMERS WHO GREW THE CROPS MADE THE PERILOUS, MONTH-LONG JOURNEY DOWNRIVER.

I HOPE WE SEE THE BOYS AGAIN — WE KNOW WE WONT SEE THE BOAT.

FLATBOATS NEVER CAME BACK. AT RIVER'S END IN NEW ORLEANS, THEY WERE SOLD FOR THEIR WOOD...

I SMELL CATFISH — IS SHE FO' MY DINNER, YVETTE?
NON-NON, BAPTISTE — YOU SMELL OUR NEW HOUSE, YES!

MANY A COTTAGE IN OLD NEW ORLEANS WAS BUILT FROM STURDY PINE AND OAK FROM A PENNSYLVANIA FOREST — WOOD FROM A BOAT THAT COULDN'T RETURN HOME.

EASE HER TO YOUR SIDE, JEB. YONDER COMES ISLAND NO. 176.

LIKE RAFTS, FLATBOATS WENT WITH THE CURRENT. THE THREE LONG "SWEEPS" WERE NO OTHER USE THAN TO KEEP THE BOAT IN THE MAIN CURRENT. NAVIGATION GUIDES, PUBLISHED AT PITTSBURGH, NUMBERED 224 ISLANDS ALONG THE WAY, AND TRIED TO KEEP TRACK OF ALL THE BENDS AND SANDBARS. BOATMEN ALWAYS HELPED A BOAT IN DISTRESS. THERE WERE MANY DANGERS.

SOMETIME AFTER THE REVOLUTION, AN UNKNOWN GENIUS NAILED A 4x4 ON THE BOTTOM OF A BATEAU.

HE'S NUTS! WHO EVER HEARD OF A KEEL ON A BOAT!!

WE COULD EVEN GO UPSTREAM! WATCH US NEXT WEEK.

KEELS MADE CONTROL OF THE BOATS POSSIBLE.

ON THESE KEELBOATS — AS THEY WERE CALLED — THE EX-INDIAN FIGHTERS BECAME "KEELERS". THEY HAVE A LARGE ROLE IN THE LOUISIANA PURCHASE STORY.

KEELBOATS

DEVELOPED IN THE PITTSBURGH VICINITY BECAME GRACEFUL CRAFT KEELBOATS RANGED FROM 40 TO 80 FEET LONG, 7 TO 10 BEAMS THEY DREW 2 FEET OF WATER WHEN LOADED.

THIS IS A BUILT-IN KEEL — IT'S AN IMPROVEMENT.

YEAH, BUT WHAT MAKES KEELBOATS GO AGAINST THE CURRENT?

THIS DOES, SON — I'LL SHOW YOU...TOMORROW.

THEY KEPT THE WEST IN THE UNION!

KEELBOATS WERE PUSHED — OR POLED — BACK UPRIVER FROM SPANISH NEW ORLEANS BY HUSKY KEELBOATMEN. WITH LUCK THEY COULD AVERAGE 15 MILES A DAY.

HEY, SENORS!

SPAIN TRIED DESPERATELY TO LURE KENTUCKY AND TENNESSEE OUT OF THE FEDERAL UNION, AND MAKE THEM A PART OF SPANISH LOUISIANA.

KEELBOATMEN were ROUGH!

WHEN THEY WEREN'T FIGHTING THE RIVER, OR THE RIVER PIRATES, OR INDIANS — **THEY FOUGHT EACH OTHER!**

GEE! THIS IS FUN! — YEP!!

I'M SCARED TO CLOSE THE PORT OF NEW ORLEANS TO 'EM.. ..AND I'M SCARED *NOT* TO.

SPANISH AUTHORITIES WERE MUCH CONCERNED ABOUT THE RESTLESS AMERICANS UPRIVER; AND THE SCRAPPY BOATMEN, WHO VISITED THEM REGULARLY, SEEMED TO CHARACTERIZE THIS ROBUST NEW WORLD NATIONALISM.

BOY! WE CAN REALLY SPEED WITH HIGH WATER. — WE MUST BE DOING 8 MILES PER HOUR – AT LEAST!

BY TREATY IN 1795, SPAIN ALLOWED AMERICANS TO BRING GOODS INTO NEW ORLEANS FOR EXPORT. SOON A MILLION DOLLARS WORTH WAS ARRIVING ANNUALLY. MOST OF IT CAME AT THIS TIME OF YEAR, WITH THE SWIFTER CURRENT OF SPRING HIGH WATER.

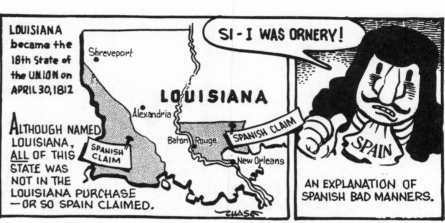

LOUISIANA became the 18th State of the UNION on APRIL 30, 1812

ALTHOUGH NAMED LOUISIANA, ALL OF THIS STATE WAS NOT IN THE LOUISIANA PURCHASE — OR SO SPAIN CLAIMED.

SI - I WAS ORNERY!

AN EXPLANATION OF SPANISH BAD MANNERS.

BOW DOWN, BUSTER.. OR I'LL TELL MY GRANDPA ON YOU!

IN 1702, ONCE PROUD AND MIGHTY SPAIN WAS FORCED TO ACCEPT THE GRANDSON OF FRENCH LOUIS XIV AS THEIR KING.

I'LL TAKE WHAT I WANT.

LATER ON, FRANCE ALSO *MADE* SPAIN TAKE LOUISIANA, TO PROTECT IT FROM THE ENGLISH.

THIS HELPS MY SELF RESPECT!

THEN ENGLAND TOOK FLORIDA AWAY FROM SPAIN. AFTER THE REVOLUTION ENGLAND GAVE IT BACK AND TOOK SOMETHING ELSE.

EVERYBODY WAS KICKING SPAIN AROUND, AND IT PUT SPAIN IN A BAD HUMOR. SO, SPAIN DECIDED TO TAKE IT OUT ON THE AMERICAN REPUBLIC, THEN VERY YOUNG.

WHO YOU KICKING?

SPAIN DIDN'T KICK AMERICANS AROUND VERY LONG. THE U.S.A. GREW STRONGER QUICKLY, AND SPAIN BECAME EVEN WEAKER.

WATCH OUT! PIRATES AROUND THE BEND!!

IN FACT, RIVER PIRATES BEGAN PREYING ON THE RICH RIVER COMMERCE. THEY BOTHERED THE BOATMEN AS MUCH AS THE SPANIARDS AT NATCHEZ AND NEW ORLEANS.

THE SPANISH MAIN HAD NOTHING ON ME — YOU'LL SEE.

ALL THE PEOPLE WHO SETTLED THE WILDERNESS WEREN'T HEROIC — THERE WERE SCOUNDRELS AND SCALAWAGS TOO. THE THIEVES AND PIRATES WHO HI-JACKED RIVER BOATS WERE AS CRUEL AND RUTHLESS AS ANY OUTLAWS.

PIRATES of the "LOUISIANA MAIN"!

I'M AS CONTEMPTIBLE AS YOU EVER WERE.

No DIFFERENTLY THAN PIRATES OF THE SPANISH MAIN, HI-JACKERS PREYED ON THE INCREASING RICHNESS OF RIVER COMMERCE. THEY WEREN'T ROMANTIC, THESE RIVER PIRATES, BUT WANTON MURDERERS OF WOMEN AND CHILDREN.

·GEE! A WOMAN! WE GOTTA HELP!

HEE! HEE! THAT GUS IS A CARD!

USUAL PRACTICE OF RIVER PIRATES WAS TO LURE A NEW ORLEANS BOUND TO THE SHORE, MURDER ALL ON BOARD, AND THEN SEE IF THE CARGO WAS WORTH LOOTING. "DEAD MEN TELL NO TALES" WAS THE MOTTO OF THE HARPES, THE MASONS, AND THE OTHERS.

No SENSIBLE PERSON TURNS OUTLAW, TO HAVE THE ODDS MILLIONS TO ONE AGAINST HIM. THOSE WHO DO ALWAYS HAVE SOME WEAKNESS IN THE HEAD.

I WAS NUTS!

OUTLAW

EVERYBODY HATES US — SO WE HATE EVERYBODY!

THE HARPE BROTHERS - BIG HARPE AND LITTLE HARPE - WERE FIRST TO TERRORIZE THE FRONTIER. THEY COULDN'T STAND THE "SHAME" OF A FATHER WHO FOUGHT WITH THE BRITISH AGAINST HIS FELLOW COLONISTS. THIS DROVE THEM CRAZY.

THE HARPES WENT HATLESS AND IN RAGS. ROBBERY WAS NEVER THEIR MOTIVE. FOR NO REASON THEY MURDERED COUNTLESS SETTLERS.

HE WAS GOING TO CAVE-IN-ROCK WHEN THEY GOT HIM.

FINALLY BIG HARPE WAS CAPTURED AND BEHEADED. HIS HEAD WAS STUCK ON A POLE BESIDE A ROAD, AND REMAINED THERE FOR YEARS. NEAR DIXON, KY. THE ROAD IS STILL CALLED "HARPE'S HEAD ROAD!"

CAVE-IN-ROCK

FIFTY MILES UP THE OHIO FROM PADUCAH WAS THIS MOST FAMOUS LAIR OF THE RIVER PIRATES.

FROM INSIDE THE CAVE PIRATES COULD SEE UP AND DOWN THE RIVER, PICK THEIR VICTIMS, AND PLAN THEIR ATTACKS.

I WUZ SCARED OF DENTISTS

THIS 40 BY 160 FOOT CAVERN KNEW ALL THE BIGSHOT PIRATES, INCLUDING SAMUEL MASON. HE WAS A GOOD CITIZEN UNTIL AGE 40, WHEN HE TURNED OUTLAW — SOME SAY ON ACCOUNT OF A TOOTH. MASON HAD ONE THAT PRO-TRUDED. WHEN HE SHUT HIS MOUTH, IT STAYED OUTSIDE. THIS UGLINESS, SO EASILY CORRECTED, WARPED HIS MIND.

SPANISH GALLEONS WERE THE FAVORED PRIZES OF SPANISH MAIN PIRATES. THEY CARRIED THE MOST.

DON'T POINT THAT THING AT ME

FLATBOATS, FOR THE SAME REASON, WERE PREFERRED BY THE RIVER PIRATES.

BESIDES, KEELBOATMEN WERE TOO ROUGH TO MESS AROUND WITH — EVEN FOR PIRATES.

AH GITS EM COMING AN GOING!

TO NEW ORLEANS.

BACK TO TENN. & KY.

FLATBOATS NEVER RETURNED FROM NEW ORLEANS, BUT FLATBOATMEN DID — BY WAY OF THE NATCHEZ TRACE. SO, RIVER PIRATES TURNED HIGHWAY-MEN TO GET A SECOND CRACK AT THESE TORMENTED OHIO VALLEY SETTLERS.

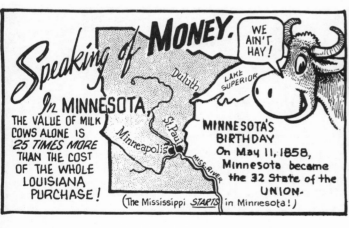

A POUND OF COFFEE, PLEASE. THIS IS THE SMALLEST I'VE GOT.

WELL.. I'LL HAVE TO GIVE YOU YOUR CHANGE IN **DUCKS**.

VERY SIMPLY, THE DEFINITION OF **MONEY** IS WHATEVER ANY MAN WILL TAKE FOR WHAT *YOU* WANT. IN THE OHIO VALLEY **ALL** THE PRODUCE OF SETTLERS WAS ACCEPTED IN STORES. **IT WAS MONEY!**

SELL IT FOR THOSE SPANISH DOLLARS.

THIS MADE EVERY MERCHANT IN THE OHIO VALLEY DEPENDENT UPON THE BOATMEN. THE ACCUMULATION OF PRODUCE HAD TO GET DOWNRIVER TO SPANISH NEW ORLEANS.

NO, SIR — YOU CAN'T MAKE MONEY LIKE THEY DID IN 1516.

I TRIED IT!!

BACK IN 1516, WHOEVER HAD A SUPPLY OF SILVER COULD MAKE HIS OWN MONEY! THAT'S WHAT COUNT SCHNICK DID, WHO LIVED IN ST. JOACHIM'S VALLEY, BOHEMIA.

THEY *ALL* COPIED ME.

THE COUNT NAMED HIS MONEY AFTER HIS VALLEY... **JOACHIM'S THALER**, IN HIS LANGUAGE. SOON ALL COINS OF SIMILAR VALUE WERE BEING CALLED THALERS — OR **DOLLARS**.

PIECES OF EIGHT WERE THE SPANISH DOLLARS. SOMETIMES THEY WERE "HOME MADE" AT REMOTE SILVER MINES IN PERU AND MEXICO.

EVEN IF SHAPED LIKE A COOKIE, SENOR — SILVER DOLLAR OKAY WITH THESE MARKS.

BUT *ALWAYS* THE SPANISH DOLLAR WAS PLAINLY MARKED WITH ITS "**8**", AND ITS "PILLARS OF HERCULES".

A Sign For The Dollar.

I THOUGHT GEORGE III HAD HORNS.

IN EARLY COLONIAL DAYS, FEW COULD READ AND WRITE. MONEY WAS RECOGNIZED BY THE **PICTURES** ON THE COINS...

BECAUSE OF THE "PILLARS OF HERCULES" ON SPANISH PIECES OF EIGHT, THEY WERE ALSO CALLED **PILLAR DOLLARS**.

$642

NOBODY KNOWS WHAT COLONIAL ACCOUNTANT FIRST IDENTIFIED SPANISH PILLAR DOLLARS IN HIS LEDGER BY AN "8" WITH TWO LINES STRUCK THROUGH IT. THIS PRACTICE SPREAD.

I GOT IT SECOND HAND!

U.S.A

IN 1792, THE U.S. ESTABLISHED ITS DOLLAR, MODELED ON THE SPANISH PIECE OF EIGHT — AND THIS SIGN FOR THE PILLAR DOLLAR BECAME THE **U.S. DOLLAR MARK!**

I SUPPOSE YOU WANT TO SELL FOR SPANISH DOLLARS, PAYABLE IN PHILADELPHIA?

SURE.. WHAT ELSE?

AS EARLY AS THE REVOLUTIONARY WAR, AMERICAN MIDDLEMEN AND BROKERS WERE ESTABLISHED IN SPANISH NEW ORLEANS.

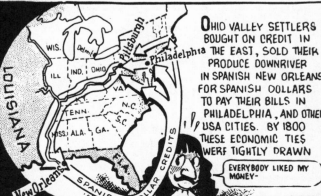

OHIO VALLEY SETTLERS BOUGHT ON CREDIT IN THE EAST, SOLD THEIR PRODUCE DOWNRIVER IN SPANISH NEW ORLEANS FOR SPANISH DOLLARS TO PAY THEIR BILLS IN PHILADELPHIA, AND OTHER USA CITIES. BY 1800 THESE ECONOMIC TIES WERE TIGHTLY DRAWN

EVERYBODY LIKED MY MONEY—

WE'RE ENGLISH. BUT WE LIKE SPANISH MONEY!

YEAH. THERE'S MORE OF IT!

IT'S EASY TO SEE HOW THIS VALLEY COMMERCE STIMULATED USE OF SPANISH DOLLARS, AND DID SO MUCH TO PUT THE DOLLAR SIGN ON THE CURRENCY OF THE U.S.A.

"I WAS SHORT OF CHANGE IN 1797."

DURING NAPOLEONIC WAR-TIME, ENGLAND STAMPED A PICTURE OF GEORGE III ON THE NECK OF SPANISH CHARLES IV, AND ISSUED PIECES OF EIGHT AS *ENGLISH MONEY*!

"Heads side", Spanish Dollar

"I WAS GETTING IT IN THE NECK FROM NAPOLEON TOO."

ENGLAND

NAPOLEON WAS FORCING KING CHARLES TO MAKE WAR ON ENGLAND IN 1797. AND, A FEW YEARS LATER, HE WAS TO TAKE LOUISIANA FROM SPAIN — A LAND MORE VALUABLE THAN ALL THE PIECES OF EIGHT EVER MADE.

"I'M TAKING THE PLEDGE, MEN! I JUST SAW TWO HEADS ON A DOLLAR!"

THE PRACTICE OF ONE NATION COUNTERSTAMPING COINS OF ANOTHER NATION, AND ISSUING THEM AS *ITS* CURRENCY HAS BEEN DONE FOR CENTURIES. BUT A SPANISH DOLLAR WITH KING GEORGE'S HEAD ON KING CHARLES' NECK WAS UNUSUAL.

"HEY, FELLOWS — GUS IS MELTING OUR BULLETS INTO DOLLARS AGAIN!"

MEANWHILE RIVER PIRATES AT CAVE-IN-ROCK WERE ACQUIRING SOME "UNUSUAL" MONEY. THEY WERE CASTING SPANISH DOLLARS OUT OF ANYTHING THAT WOULD MELT.

"JEEPERS! WHO MIXED UP OUR REAL DOUGH WITH THE MONKEY MONEY!"

EARLY MISSISSIPPI VALLEY COUNTER-FEITERS DIDN'T HAVE TO BE VERY EXPERT, BECAUSE THE REAL MONEY WASN'T VERY EXPERTLY MADE

ALTHOUGH COUNTERFEITERS DIDN'T HAVE TO BE EXPERT TO MAKE PASSABLE MONEY DURING KEELBOATING YEARS ON THE RIVER, THEIRS WAS AN UNHEALTHY BUSINESS. THE BOATMEN, ONCE SWINDLED, WENT GUNNING FOR THEM!

"SLIP ME A PHONY DIME, WILL YA!"

THERE WASN'T MUCH PERCENTAGE IN BEING A CRIMINAL, WHEN THE LAW-ABIDING CITIZENS PLAYED AS ROUGH AS THE KEELBOATMEN DID WHEN THEY CAUGHT YOU.

"COME ON, ANYBODY — EXCEPT MIKE!"

EVERY KEELBOATMAN CONSIDERED HIM-SELF THE FIGHTIN'EST, SHOOTIN'EST GUY ON THE RIVER — EXCEPT *ONE*. ALL AGREED **MIKE FINK** WAS NO. 1. (Meet Mike)

"IT'S A BOY, MRS. FINK!"

MIKE FINK WAS BORN IN ONE OF THE SEVERAL LOG CABINS THAT WAS PITTSBURGH IN 1770.

"HECK! I MISSED THAT SQUIRREL—THAT IS, I MISSED HIS LEFT EYE."

MIKE NEVER KNEW ANY OTHER LIFE THAN THE HARDSHIPS AND VIOLENCE OF THE FRONTIER. HE HAD HIS OWN RIFLE AT AGE 12, AND HE COULD SHOOT IT, TOO!

"GEE! *THAT* LOOKS LIKE FUN!"

WHEN MIKE WAS 17, HE WAS AN EXPERIENCED INDIAN FIGHTER, AND THE BEST SHOT ON THE PITTSBURGH FRONTIER WHERE ALL WERE MARKSMEN. HE GOT BORED WITH INDIAN FIGHTING, AND TURNED KEELBOATMAN.

NOW LET ME TELL A STORY ABOUT MIKE!

MIKE FINK WAS GREAT — AT SHOOTING, FIGHTING, BOATING, EVERYTHING. BUT YARNS ABOUT HIM SPUN BY ADMIRING KEELBOATMEN WERE GREATER. MIKE FINK BECAME A LIVING LEGEND!

YOU FORGOT YOU WERE A LEGEND, MIKE.

NOW HE TELLS ME!

SHOOTING THE CUP WAS THE FAVORED SPORT OF MIKE AND HIS FRIENDS. WINNER WAS THE MAN WHOSE SHOT WENT THROUGH THE TIN CUP *ABOVE* THE WHISKEY IN IT. ONE DAY MIKE WAS SHOOTING WITH A FELLOW WHOM HE SUSPECTED OF TRYING TO STEAL HIS GIRL. MIKE "ACCIDENTALLY" SHOT HIM THROUGH THE HEAD.

A FRIEND OF THE DECEASED KILLED MIKE FOR THIS. NOBODY EVER BELIEVED MIKE MISSED THAT SHOT EITHER.

Henry Shreve was a legend too -

HENRY SHREVE WAS RAISED ON THE BANKS OF THE YOUGHIOGHENY NEAR PITTSBURGH. THE STRANGE PARADE OF RIVER CRAFT FASCINATED THE LITTLE BOY...

HE SAYS HIS NAME IS SHREVE.

WHEN HE WAS 21, HENRY SHREVE BUILT HIS OWN KEELBOAT, AND CAST OFF FOR ST. LOUIS TO TRADE FOR FURS. ON THIS TRIP, IT WAS QUITE POSSIBLE FOR YOUNG CAPTAIN SHREVE TO HAVE ENCOUNTERED THE FAMOUS MIKE FINK. SHREVE WAS COMMENCING A CAREER ON THE RIVER MORE FABULOUS THAN EVEN MIKE'S.

I HAD A BIG JOB.

ON MAY 25, 1801 WM. C. C. CLAIBORNE WAS NAMED GOVERNOR OF THE TERRITORY OF MISSISSIPPI, COMPRISING THE PRESENT STATES OF ALABAMA AND MISSISSIPPI. CLAIBORNE WAS AGE 26.

TENNESSEE / GEORGIA / SPANISH FLORIDA

SO MONTHS LATER, YOUNG CLAIBORNE WAS ALSO GOVERNOR OF ALL THIS — MORE THAN HALF THE U.S.!

WHEN I WAS YOUNG, MY LEADERS WERE, TOO. THERE WAS HENRY SHREVE..

UNITED STATES AFTER 1803

HE *INVENTED* THE RIVER STEAMBOAT!

THERE'S A LOT OF CONTROVERSY SURROUNDING HENRY SHREVE, THE PENNSYLVANIA QUAKER BOY, WHO WAS A KEELBOAT SKIPPER AT AGE 21.

BAH! THE STEAMBOAT WAS THE RESULT OF GRADUAL IMPROVEMENT!

SOME HISTORIANS INSIST HE DESIGNED THE KIND OF STEAMBOAT THAT FLOATED ON *TOP* THE RIVER LIKE A BIG CANOE. OTHER HISTORIANS DENY IT.

LOOK! A STEAMBOAT FROM NEW ORLEANS — THE *FIRST* ONE!

BUT ALL AGREE THAT HENRY SHREVE, WHEN HE WAS 29, WAS THE FIRST CAPTAIN TO SUCCESSFULLY RUN A STEAMBOAT *UPRIVER* FROM NEW ORLEANS TO LOUISVILLE, KENTUCKY!

To be sure, steamboats and steamboatmen belong to the years *following* the Louisiana Purchase. But experiments with steamboats, and the experience of boatmen commenced long before 1803.

We just got hold of some puny Indians, Mr. Fitch.

?

I built a **ship** — not a boat..

In 1787, John Fitch invented a boat driven by mechanical canoe paddles. But top speed of this 12-Indian power steamer was only 2 M.P.H. Finally, John Fitch took poison in disgust.

Robert Fulton, 19 years after Fitch, achieved the first practical steamer. He tried to run his model on the shallow Mississippi. But he wasn't as river-wise as Henry Shreve.

Henry knows all about me.

OLD MAN RIVER

Henry Shreve had 7 years experience on the river as a keelboat skipper, before he took his first steamboat down the river to New Orleans.

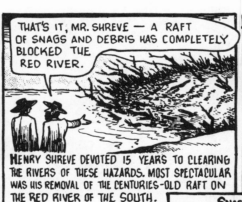

Put the engine on the deck...can't you give it some upper decks?

Well..it's never been done before.

This was the "Enterprise", a deep draft Fulton-type boat. With the aid of spring high water, Shreve steamed it upriver to Louisville.

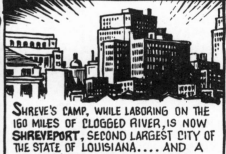

Riverwise Shreve surely must have influenced design of river steamers into the flat bottomed, towering craft that became the world-famous Mississippi steamboat. Anyway, the first new model was built for *him*.

Missouri River Scene...

Great curse of river navigation were the **snags**, huge stumps and trees that could rip open the bottom of a steamboat. Snags were worse on the western rivers, in Louisiana Purchase Territory.

That's it, Mr. Shreve — a raft of snags and debris has completely blocked the Red River.

Henry Shreve devoted 15 years to clearing the rivers of these hazards. Most spectacular was his removal of the centuries-old raft on the Red River of the South.

Shreve's camp, while laboring on the 160 miles of clogged river, is now **Shreveport**, second largest city of the state of Louisiana..... and a monument to Henry Shreve.

Snags plagued Uncle Sam in *1801* too.

What about our treaty with **Spain**?

In 1801, it was learned the rumors were true! Spain had, indeed, ceded Louisiana back to France! What would the Ohio Valley do?

ENGLISH POLICY

NAPOLEON'S AMBITIONS

SPANISH PRIDE

Snags now endangered the future of the United States. If the free navigation of the Mississippi was denied the frontier states they would surely secede. "No protection, no allegiance" said the Kentuckians. American diplomacy rose magnificently to the occasion.

We'll see you at the birthday parties!

Next

But oo it is an American custom to pause and observe anniversaries. Before Jefferson, and his ministers, tackle Napoleon, come three historic birthdays!

HI, JUNIOR!

THEY SPEARHEADED THE MARCH OF THE U.S. ACROSS A CONTINENT!

IT'S UP TO ME!

KENTUCKY AND TENNESSEE ARE TWINS ALMOST — THEY HAVE THE SAME BIRTHDAY, BUT 4 YEARS APART. KENTUCKY BECAME THE 15th STATE ON JUNE 1st, 1792. TENNESSEE ENTERED IN 1796.

LEFT TO PROTECT THEMSELVES FROM FRENCH, ENGLISH, SPANISH, AND INDIAN ATTACKS, SMALL WONDER THESE STATES BRED FIGHTING MEN.

KENTA-KE.. OR "MEADOW LAND" TO YOU, PALEFACE.

CITY LIMITS TINNASE

THAT'S ME ALL OVER!

BOTH KENTUCKY AND TENNESSEE HAVE INDIAN NAMES. THE IROQUOIS WORD NICELY DESCRIBES THE BLUE GRASS STATE. BUT TENNESSEE COMES FROM THE NAME OF A CHEROKEE VILLAGE, AND ALL THE CHEROKEES HAVE FORGOTTEN WHAT "TINNASE" MEANS!

ACTUALLY, MORE THAN HALF THE 50 STATES HAVE INDIAN NAMES — AND TWO STATES HAVE NAMES DERIVED FROM THE SAME INDIAN WORD!

WISCONSIN BIRTHDAY MAY 29, 1848

SPELLING - BAH! I'M AN ARTIST!!

THE STATE'S INDIAN NAME COMES FROM THE WISCONSIN RIVER, WHICH THE FRENCH RECORDED.. "OUISCONSINK."

NOT PART OF THE LOUISIANA PURCHASE, BUT HISTORIC PASSAGE INTO THE MISSISSIPPI VALLEY WAS THE FOX RIVER PORTAGE TO THE OUISCONSINK (WISCONSIN).

IN 1715, A FRENCH MAP ARTIST MISSPELLED OUISCONSINK INTO OUARICONSINT — AND DIVIDED THE WORD AS SHOWN HERE. THE NEXT WRITER CALLED THE RIVER "OUARICON."

Meet the next writer.

Major Robert Rogers

WAS A GREAT INDIAN FIGHTER, BUT VERY UNRELIABLE IN MONEY MATTERS, AND WITH HISTORICAL FACTS.

NO!

BUT KING...I SAW OUARICON ON A MAP!

OREGON!!

IMMIGRANT

THE MAJOR WAS THE WRITER WHO SPELLED THE WISCONSIN RIVER OUARICON. HE ALSO DECLARED IT WAS THE NORTHWEST PASSAGE!

A Concise Account of North America By Major Rogers

THE MAJOR WAS IN LONDON VAINLY TRYING TO GET KING GEORGE TO PUT UP $80,821.22 FOR A ROGERS EXPEDITION THROUGH THIS "NORTHWEST PASSAGE".

Travels Through Interior Of America BY CARVER

LATER, JONATHON CARVER WAS, IN TURN, INFLUENCED BY ROGERS' BOOK. CARVER ALTERED OUARICON INTO OREGON. HIS BOOK WAS A BEST-SELLER — AND IT "SOLD" OREGON TOO!

YONDER'S OREGON— IF WE EVER FIND IT.

OREGON— A WORD SO STRANGELY COME BY— BECAME THE NAME OF THE PACIFIC NORTHWEST BEFORE THE REGION WAS EVER EXPLORED.

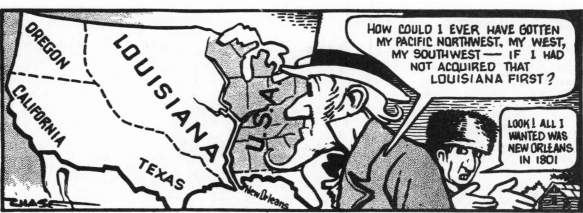

HOW COULD I EVER HAVE GOTTEN MY PACIFIC NORTHWEST, MY WEST, MY SOUTHWEST — IF I HAD NOT ACQUIRED THAT LOUISIANA FIRST?

LOOK! ALL I WANTED WAS NEW ORLEANS IN 1801

OREGON
CALIFORNIA
LOUISIANA
TEXAS
U.S.A.
New Orleans

NAPOLEON TAKES OVER LOUISIANA

WHO IS THIS FELLOW NAPOLEON?

YEAH. WHAT INDIANS DID HE EVER FIGHT?

SIGNIFICANCE OF THE LOUISIANA PURCHASE: IT MADE POSSIBLE A UNITED STATES STRETCHING FROM SEA TO SEA —— BUT **THAT** WASN'T IMPORTANT TO THE OHIO VALLEY FOLKS IN 1801.

THE OHIO VALLEY'S ECONOMIC LIFE *DEPENDED* UPON FREE NAVIGATION OF THE MISSISSIPPI, AND USE OF THE PORT OF NEW ORLEANS. "WOULD THIS NAPOLEON STOP THAT?" THE SETTLERS WANTED TO KNOW.

THIS FELLOW NAPOLEON!

FASTER, STORK— FASTER!

CORSICA

NAPOLEON WAS BORN ON AN ISLAND, AND DIED ON AN ISLAND... BUT HIS CAREER RESHAPED WHOLE CONTINENTS, INCLUDING CONTINENTAL UNITED STATES.

I CAME FAST, TOO.

ST. HELENA

TODAY ON ST. HELENA A GIANT TURTLE, WHO KNEW NAPOLEON, *STILL* CRAWLS AROUND THAT REMOTE ISLAND...

I'M NO NAPOLEON — BUT **I'M STILL HERE!**

HOWEVER, THERE WAS NOTHING TURTLE-LIKE IN NAPOLEON'S PROGRESS BETWEEN CORSICA AND ST. HELENA... IN 37 YEARS HE DID ALL HE DID.

HE ISN'T PRETTY— SO WHAT! MAYBE HE'LL HAVE TALENT.

THE YEAR NAPOLEON WAS BORN WAS ALSO THE DATE OF THE FIRST ENGLISH-SPEAKING SETTLEMENT IN THE MISSISSIPPI RIVER VALLEY— LASALLE'S LOUISIANA.

THIS WAS THE SETTLING OF WESTERN PENNSYLVANIA AROUND PITTSBURGH. 10,000 SETTLERS MOVED HERE BEFORE NAPOLEON'S FIFTH BIRTHDAY.

WHEN HE WAS NINE, NAPOLEON LEFT CORSICA FOR SCHOOL IN FRANCE. AT THIS SAME TIME, GEORGE ROGERS CLARK WAS CONQUERING THE NORTHWEST FOR THE UNITED STATES.

SIT DOWN, NAPOLEON - YOU'RE ROCKING THE BOAT!

LOUISIANA PURCHASE

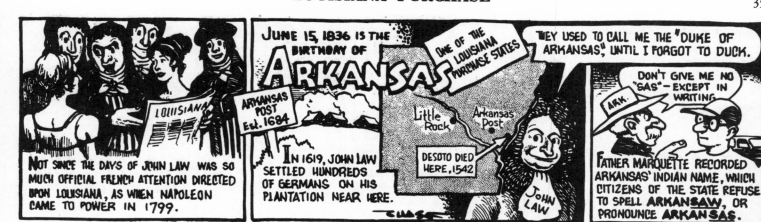

NOT SINCE THE DAYS OF JOHN LAW WAS SO MUCH OFFICIAL FRENCH ATTENTION DIRECTED UPON LOUISIANA, AS WHEN NAPOLEON CAME TO POWER IN 1799.

JUNE 15, 1836 IS THE BIRTHDAY OF ARKANSAS

ONE OF THE LOUISIANA PURCHASE STATES

ARKANSAS POST Est. 1684

IN 1619, JOHN LAW SETTLED HUNDREDS OF GERMANS ON HIS PLANTATION NEAR HERE.

Little Rock / Arkansas Post / DESOTO DIED HERE, 1542 / JOHN LAW

THEY USED TO CALL ME THE "DUKE OF ARKANSAS" UNTIL I FORGOT TO DUCK.

DON'T GIVE ME NO "GAS" — EXCEPT IN WRITING. / ARK.

FATHER MARQUETTE RECORDED ARKANSAS' INDIAN NAME, WHICH CITIZENS OF THE STATE REFUSE TO SPELL ARKANSAW, OR PRONOUNCE ARKANSAS.

INDIAN GIVER!! / WE WANT LOUISIANA BACK! / SPAIN

AFTER THE FRENCH REVOLUTION, THE PATRIOTS WANTED SPAIN TO GIVE LOUISIANA BACK TO FRANCE. THE PATRIOTS CLAIMED THE KING HAD GIVEN LOUISIANA AWAY. NOW, THE KING WAS DEAD.

WHAT LOUISIANA COST THE USA / WHAT LOUISIANA COST SPAIN

SPAIN SHOULD HAVE BEEN GLAD TO BE RID OF LOUISIANA. DURING 37 YEARS OF RULE, SPAIN SPENT MORE MAINTAINING LOUISIANA THAN THE U.S. PAID TO BUY THE COUNTRY OUTRIGHT!

NEW ORLEANS

TO BEGIN WITH, FRENCHMEN IN NEW ORLEANS KICKED OUT THE FIRST SPANISH GOVERNOR. SPAIN HAD TO GO TO THE EXPENSE OF SUPPRESSING A REVOLUTION . . .

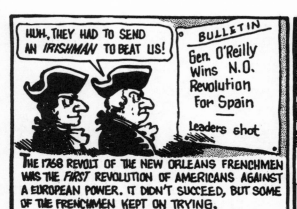

HUH, THEY HAD TO SEND AN IRISHMAN TO BEAT US!

BULLETIN / Gen. O'Reilly Wins N.O. Revolution For Spain — Leaders shot

THE 1768 REVOLT OF THE NEW ORLEANS FRENCHMEN WAS THE FIRST REVOLUTION OF AMERICANS AGAINST A EUROPEAN POWER. IT DIDN'T SUCCEED, BUT SOME OF THE FRENCHMEN KEPT ON TRYING.

I DIDN'T HAVE ANY INSURANCE, EITHER... / SPAIN

ALSO, FIRES IN 1788 AND 1794 ALMOST BURNED UP NEW ORLEANS. MORE EXPENSE! SPAIN HAD TO PRACTICALLY REBUILD THE CITY.

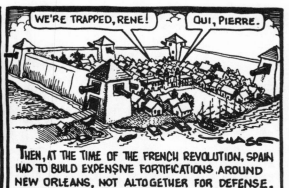

WE'RE TRAPPED, RENE! / OUI, PIERRE.

THEN, AT THE TIME OF THE FRENCH REVOLUTION, SPAIN HAD TO BUILD EXPENSIVE FORTIFICATIONS AROUND NEW ORLEANS, NOT ALTOGETHER FOR DEFENSE, BUT TO KEEP RESTLESS FRENCHMEN INSIDE, TOO!

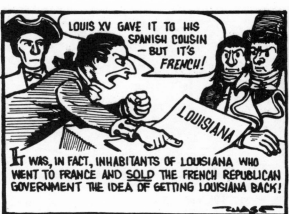

LOUIS XV GAVE IT TO HIS SPANISH COUSIN — BUT IT'S FRENCH! / LOUISIANA

IT WAS, IN FACT, INHABITANTS OF LOUISIANA WHO WENT TO FRANCE AND SOLD THE FRENCH REPUBLICAN GOVERNMENT THE IDEA OF GETTING LOUISIANA BACK!

WE ENDED UP ON THE SAME SIDE!

JUST AS OHIO VALLEY SETTLERS PESTERED THE U.S. GOVERNMENT UNTIL LOUISIANA WAS PURCHASED, THESE FRENCH LOUISIANIANS KEPT BEHIND THE FRENCH GOVERNMENT, AND GOT RESULTS!

WE WANT LOUISIANA!

FINALLY, THE FRENCH POLITICIANS — LIKE ALL POLITICIANS — BEGAN TO THINK THE RETROCESSION OF LOUISIANA WAS THEIR IDEA.

Meet Talleyrand.

TALLEYRAND

I ONLY WANTED TO BE ON THE WINNING SIDE..

...HE WAS A GOOD POLITICIAN TO HAVE ON YOUR SIDE IN A TIGHT SPOT, EXCEPT IT WAS HARD TO KNOW WHEN TALLEYRAND WOULD *CHANGE* SIDES!

HE DOUBLE-CROSSED THE ARISTOCRACY FOR THE REPUBLICAN PATRIOTS, THEN HE DOUBLE-CROSSED THEM FOR NAPOLEON, WHOM HE LATER DOUBLE-CROSSED FOR THE ARISTOCRATS AGAIN.

HMM-M, I EVEN DOUBLE-CROSSED MY *T's!*

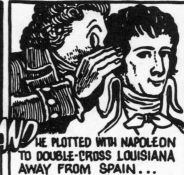

AND HE PLOTTED WITH NAPOLEON TO DOUBLE-CROSS LOUISIANA AWAY FROM SPAIN...

CHASE

NAPOLEON MEANT TROUBLE FOR THE U.S. WHEN HE ACQUIRED LOUISIANA, BUT THE TROUBLE WAS NOT ALL OF NAPOLEON'S MAKING.

FIRST THERE WAS CITIZEN GENET, FRENCH REVOLUTIONARY MINISTER TO THE U.S. OPENLY, HE TRIED TO STIR UP A WAR BETWEEN AMERICANS AND SPAIN...

HE'S *SOME* AMBASSADOR!

COME ON! LET'S *YOU* GO CAPTURE LOUISIANA FOR *ME!*

XYZ AFFAIR

THEN, TALLEYRAND ALMOST PROVOKED WAR BETWEEN THE U.S. AND FRANCE!

WHILE TALLEYRAND WAS IN THE PROCESS OF DOUBLE-CROSSING THE FRENCH ARISTOCRACY FOR THE REVOLUTIONISTS, HE WAS LIVING IN LONDON FOR SAFETY. BUT SUSPICIOUS JOHN BULL KICKED HIM OUT. TALLEYRAND WAS EXILED TO THE U.S.A.

JUST REMEMBER — I WAS DOUBLE-CROSSED FIRST!

BUT LET'S BE FAIR WITH TALLEYRAND... DURING A MOST UNHAPPY CHILDHOOD, HE WAS DROPPED BY HIS NURSE. THIS ACCIDENT LEFT HIM (1) PERMANENTLY LAME, AND (2) PERMANENTLY MAD AT *EVERYBODY!*

HE'LL BE AN ALLY OF ENGLAND, IF I DON'T DO SOMETHING ABOUT IT.

TALLEYRAND NEVER LOST HIS APPETITE FOR BITING THE HAND THAT FED HIM. WHILE ENJOYING POLITICAL SANCTUARY IN THE U.S., HE PLANNED TO DOUBLE-CROSS UNCLE SAM.

WAIT'LL YOU TRY TO GET A FRENCH TREATY

IN 1796—AFTER OVER TWO YEARS IN THE U.S.—TALLEYRAND RETURNED TO FRANCE. HE HAD SEEN FRENCH MEDDLING IN U.S. AFFAIRS RESULT IN AMERICAN TREATIES WITH ENGLAND AND SPAIN—BOTH ENEMIES OF FRANCE.

JAY TREATY

ENGLAND • USA •

Chicago.. at this time.

BY THE JAY TREATY, ENGLAND FINALLY VACATED DETROIT, CHICAGO, AND OTHER POSTS IN THE NORTHWEST. AT LEAST, IT AVOIDED A U.S. WAR WITH ENGLAND.

Treaty of San Lorenzo

SPAIN • USA •

AND THE SPANISH TREATY WAS THE ONE THAT FINALLY GRANTED OHIO VALLEY BOATMEN FREE NAVIGATION OF THE MISSISSIPPI, AND USE OF THE PORT OF NEW ORLEANS.

CHASE

THE DIRECTORY GOVERNMENT OF FRANCE WAS ESPECIALLY MAD ABOUT THE JAY TREATY, AND BEGAN SEIZING MERCHANT SHIPS OF THE UNITED STATES...

THUS EXISTED IN 1797, A STATE OF UNDECLARED WAR BETWEEN FRANCE AND THE U.S. PRESIDENT JOHN ADAMS SENT THREE ENVOYS TO PARIS FOR PEACE TALKS.

TALLEYRAND, NOW FRENCH FOREIGN MINISTER, ASSIGNED THREE FRENCHMEN TO GO DICKER WITH THE AMERICANS. HISTORY KNOWS THESE FRENCHMEN BEST AS MR. X, MR. Y, AND MR. Z

THE AMERICAN ENVOYS WERE SHOCKED AT THE CONDITIONS LAID DOWN BY MESSRS. X, Y, AND Z AT THE PARIS PEACE TALKS.

TALLEYRAND, IN TURN, WAS SHOCKED AT THE REACTIONS OF THE AMERICANS. HE HAD BEEN SHAKING DOWN EVERY NATION IN EUROPE THAT WANTED TO CURRY FAVOR WITH FRANCE.

THIS XYZ AFFAIR MADE THE AMERICAN PEOPLE FIGHTING MAD, HOWEVER

AMONG PREPARATIONS THE AROUSED UNITED STATES MADE FOR A WAR WITH FRANCE WAS THE ESTABLISHMENT OF A NAVY. ON MAY 3, 1798 BENJ. STODDARD OF MARYLAND BECAME FIRST SECRETARY OF NAVY.

NAPOLEON ARRIVED FROM EGYPT JUST IN TIME TO BE TALLEYRAND'S BOY IN A COUP D'ÉTAT HE WAS PLOTTING.

IT WAS, IN FACT, TALLEYRAND'S INTRIGUE THAT BROUGHT NAPOLEON TO POWER. TALLEYRAND RATHER THOUGHT HE WOULD RULE THROUGH NAPOLEON.

...BUT NAPOLEON TURNED OUT TO BE NAPOLEON!

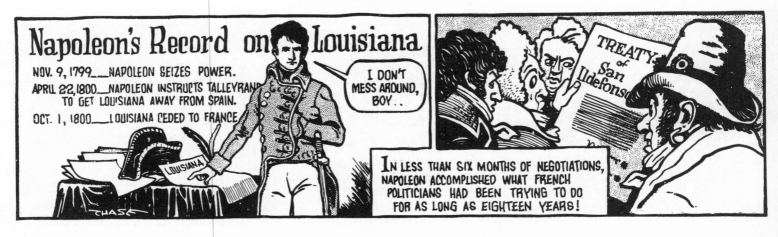

Napoleon's Record on Louisiana

NOV. 9, 1799—NAPOLEON SEIZES POWER.

APRIL 22, 1800—NAPOLEON INSTRUCTS TALLEYRAND TO GET LOUISIANA AWAY FROM SPAIN.

OCT. 1, 1800—LOUISIANA CEDED TO FRANCE.

I DON'T MESS AROUND, BOY...

TREATY of San Ildefonso

IN LESS THAN SIX MONTHS OF NEGOTIATIONS, NAPOLEON ACCOMPLISHED WHAT FRENCH POLITICIANS HAD BEEN TRYING TO DO FOR AS LONG AS EIGHTEEN YEARS!

OUI! IT WOULD BE NICE!

AS EARLY AS 1783, FRENCH COLONIAL POLICY-MAKERS DREAMED OF GETTING LOUISIANA BACK FROM SPAIN. PROSPECT OF EXCLUSIVE TRADE WITH THE NEW UNITED STATES, FRANCE'S ALLY THEN, WAS BEHIND THESE DREAMS.

BUT WE WONT BE LONG!

OHIO VALLEY

IN 1783, OHIO VALLEY TRADE HAD NOT YET MADE THE MISSISSIPPI AND NEW ORLEANS COMMERCIALLY IMPORTANT. THEN, SPAIN PROBABLY WOULD HAVE GIVEN THE COLONY BACK TO FRANCE.

LOUISIANA IS RIGHTFULLY OURS!

BUT, CAME THE FRENCH REVOLUTION. EGGED ON BY THOSE DELEGATIONS FROM LOUISIANA, THE REVOLUTIONARY GOVERNMENT ENGAGED IN SEVERAL YEARS OF WARLIKE BLUSTER—THEY WERE GOING TO CONQUER LOUISIANA.

INSTEAD OF FIGHTING YOU FOR LOUISIANA—HOW ABOUT JUST GIVING IT TO US?

IN APRIL OF 1795, THE FRENCH REPUBLICAN GOVERNMENT MADE ITS FIRST EFFORT TO RECOVER LOUISIANA PEACEABLY, BY RETROCESSION.

THE GUILLOTINE IS OUT OF STYLE, BUT EXILE TO THE LOUISIANA WILDERNESS WOULD BE GOOD ENOUGH FOR TRAITORS

YEAH, BUT IS THAT HUMANE?

OTHER THAN THE PROPAGANDA OF THOSE DELEGATIONS FROM NEW ORLEANS, IT'S NOT CLEAR WHY THE FRENCH REPUBLIC WANTED LOUISIANA—ONE EXPLANATION WAS THAT IT WOULD BE USEFUL FOR STASHING AWAY POLITICAL EXILES!

MAÑANA.. MAÑANA..

THAT MEANS TOMORROW.

..BUT HE SAID IT YESTERDAY, TOO.

BUT, NOW SPAIN WAS BEGINNING TO ENJOY SOME OF THE BENEFITS OF TRADE FROM THE OHIO VALLEY. FOR FIVE YEARS SPANISH MINISTERS PUT OFF THE FRENCH, ALMOST FROM DAY TO DAY.

WHAT TO DO ABOUT LOUISIANA ??

I DON'T EVEN KNOW WHAT TO DO ABOUT SPAIN!

SPAIN WAS WEAK IN THE CLOSING YEARS OF THE 18th. CENTURY; AND CHARLES IV, HER KING, HAD DIFFICULTY MAKING UP HIS MIND ABOUT MOST ANYTHING.

SHE'S NO BEAUTY—BUT SHE'S THE BOSS.

STRONGER WAS HIS QUEEN, MARIA LOUSA OF PARMA. MANUEL GODOY, SPANISH MINISTER WHO DICKERED WITH THE FRENCH WAS THE QUEEN'S MAN, NOT THE KING'S.

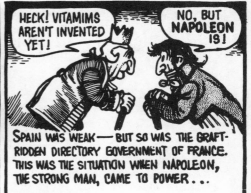

HECK! VITAMIMS AREN'T INVENTED YET!

NO, BUT NAPOLEON IS!

SPAIN WAS WEAK—BUT SO WAS THE GRAFT-RIDDEN DIRECTORY GOVERNMENT OF FRANCE. THIS WAS THE SITUATION WHEN NAPOLEON, THE STRONG MAN, CAME TO POWER...

WE'LL FINESSE WITH A QUEEN IN THIS GAME, TALLEYRAND...

HERE'S THE DEAL, QUEENIE - SPAIN GIVES ME LOUISIANA, AND I GO CONQUER SOME LAND IN ITALY FOR YOUR BROTHER, FERDIE.

I'LL SHAKE ON THAT, NAPOLEON.

IT'S EASY — WHEN YOU'RE NAPOLEON!

NAPOLEON SIZED UP THE SPANISH COURT RIGHT. THE QUEEN WAS BOSS: AND HER BROTHER, FERDINAND, DUKE OF PARMA, DIDN'T HAVE ENOUGH LAND IN ITALY TO SUPPORT HIM.

AS SIMPLE AS THIS NAPOLEON RECOVERED OVER 800,000 SQUARE MILES FOR A FEW THOUSAND ACRES OF SOMEBODY ELSE'S LAND IN ITALY

LOOK AT IT THIS WAY, KING. ALL I GET IS LOUISIANA, BUT YOU GET YOUR BROTHER-IN-LAW OUTTA THE HOUSE.

YEAH!!

CHARLES IV

THE TREATY OF SAN ILDEFONSO PROVIDED THAT NAPOLEON GET LOUISIANA, AND THE DUKE OF PARMA GET MORE BACKYARD FOR HIS ESTATE IN ITALY. ACTUALLY, NEITHER NAPOLEON NOR THE DUKE GOT *ANYTHING*.

THE TREATY WAS VERY SECRET. THE DUKE OF PARMA DIED WITHOUT EVER FINDING THE LAND HE WAS SUPPOSED TO GET.

Uncle Sam gets France's pants - next

UNLIKE PREVIOUS FRENCH GOVERNMENTS, NAPOLEON HAD REAL PLANS FOR LOUISIANA. SECRETLY, HE BEGAN SCHEMING A FRENCH COLONIAL EMPIRE. BUT THE BRITISH NAVY, AN HEROIC NEGRO, AND SOME MOSQUITOS HAD OTHER PLANS —— AS WE SHALL SEE ...

LET ANY WHO MAY BE UNCONVINCED THAT THE LOUISIANA PURCHASE WAS NOT THE BEGINNING OF U.S. NATIONAL IMPORTANCE, BE REASSURED BY **UNCLE SAM**

AS THE SYMBOLIC FIGURE OF THE USA, I BROKE INTO PRINT FIRST, AFTER THE PURCHASE OF LOUISIANA ...

FROM FRANCE, UNCLE SAM NOT ONLY GOT LOUISIANA, BUT ALL HIS CLOTHING TOO!

I'LL TELL YOU WHERE FRANCE GOT 'EM.

The **FRENCH REVOLUTION** WAS A REVOLT AGAINST THE HATED ARISTOCRACY, AND EVERYTHING ABOUT THEM... **INCLUDING THEIR FANCY CLOTHES.**

THE ROUGH ATTIRE OF THE LOWER CLASSES BECAME THE <u>STYLE</u> IN FRANCE.

I HATE YOU, AND I HATE YOUR BREECHES, TOO.

I'VE GOT SOME *SPECIAL* IDEAS FOR THE LADIES!

WE <u>HOPE</u> SO!

JACQUES LOUIS **DAVID** ∨

THIS CELEBRATED FRENCH ARTIST WAS ORDERED BY THE DIRECTORY GOVERNMENT TO DESIGN A NATIONAL DRESS FOR FRANCE.

JACQUES LOUIS **DAVID** PAINTED POWERFUL HISTORICAL PICTURES THAT KEPT FRENCH EMOTIONS STEAMED UP OVER THEIR REVOLUTION...

GR-R! LET'S GO FIND SOME MORE PESKY ARISTOCRATS!

GEE!

AS DESIGNER OF A NATIONAL FRENCH DRESS, HE PUT MEN IN LONG PANTS AND PLAIN COATS. THAT IS *STILL* THE STYLE FOR **ALL MEN.**

WHEE! I FEEL JUST LIKE A GREEK!

I JUST FEEL COLD!

AND, MORE THAN ANYBODY, DAVID INFLUENCED THE GREEK REVIVAL IN ALL THE ARTS... INCLUDING WOMEN'S FASHIONS.

THIS REVOLUTION IS GETTING EXPENSIVE..

ALTHOUGH THE FRENCH REVOLUTION STANDARDIZED MEN'S CLOTHES, IT STARTED THE CUSTOM OF FASHIONABLE WOMEN CHANGING *THEIR* STYLE WHEN OTHER WOMEN APPEARED DRESSED LIKE THEM!

BUT.. *WHY* ISN'T IT CHILLY?

BECAUSE, SILLY— IT'S **STYLISH!**

OBJECT OF THE FIRST FRENCH NATIONAL DRESS WAS SIMPLICITY, AND NOTHING COULD HAVE BEEN SIMPLER THAN DAVID'S GREEK GOWNS — EXCEPT **NOTHING.**

IN THE GARDEN, MEN — IT'S FOR THE BIRDS!

Royal Tub

NOW, BOTH MEN AND WOMEN COMMENCED TO BATHE REGULARLY, WHICH IS MORE THAN THE ARISTOCRACY EVER DID. IT IS SAID THAT THE ONLY BATHTUB IN VERSAILLES PALACE WAS ONCE MOVED TO THE GARDEN — FOR A FOUNTAIN.

YEP, I STILL HAVE MY OLD FRENCH CLOTHES — AND MY OLD FRENCH COLONY, **TOO!**

SINCE 1803, MEN'S CLOTHES HAVE CHANGED TO BECOME EVEN PLAINER. BUT UNCLE SAM STICKS TO THE OUTFIT IN STYLE WHEN HE BOUGHT LOUISIANA.

WYOMING - THAT GOT ITS NAME IN PENNSYLVANIA.

WASH. OREGON OREGON TRAIL CALIFORNIA TRAIL FORNIA UTAH ILL. IND. OHIO PENN. W.VA. KY. VA. TENN. N.C. MISS. ALA. GA S.C. TEXAS FLORIDA

JULY 10, 1890 IS THE BIRTHDAY OF WYOMING, THE FAR-WEST LOUISIANA PURCHASE STATE. ON THE OREGON TRAIL TO THE PACIFIC COAST.

THE FRENCH REVOLUTION THAT STANDARDIZED CLOTHES, RESULTED IN READY-TO-WEAR SHOPS. AFTER 1791, ONE COULD BUY CLOTHES ALREADY MADE.

I'LL DIE FOR MY EMPEROR, BUT I **WON'T** WEAR A PINK SUIT FOR HIM.

NAPOLEON, WHEN HE WAS EMPEROR, TRIED TO REVIVE GAY COLORS FOR MEN'S COURT ATTIRE. INSTEAD, FORMAL DRESS FOR MEN BECAME, AND HAS REMAINED, **BLACK.**

I CAN'T LOSE! EITHER I GET BACK SANTO DOMINGO, OR I DON'T GET BACK THAT BROTHER-IN-LAW!

BUT, ON OCT. 1, 1801 CAME PEACE WITH ENGLAND, AND NAPOLEON COMMENCED HIS ATTEMPT TO REVIVE FRENCH COLONIAL POWER. ON NOV. 22, HE ORDERED HIS BROTHER-IN-LAW TO GO RECONQUER SANTO DOMINGO, WHICH HAD REVOLTED.

In December of 1801, 54 ships with 20,000 veteran troops left France for Santo Domingo. Napoleon determined to make short work of a revolt in that island.

"Let 'em think we're friends —then!"

With treachery and deceit, Napoleon planned to reenslave the negroes of Santo Domingo!

"Maybe we'll die... but we'll die free men."

But Napoleon and his brother-in-law, General Leclerc, in command of the expedition, reckoned without the fighting spirits of men who had won freedom, and their great leader.

Toussaint Louverture

is one of the world's great men. In French Santo Domingo, he led his fellow negro slaves to freedom and independence, and he beat off Napoleon's attempt to reenslave his people. Actually, he *forced* Napoleon to sell Louisiana!

LOUISIANA FOR SALE
On account of Toussaint
APPLY NAPOLEON

"With slave labor, we clean up..."

PROFITS...

For long years before the French Revolution, Santo Domingo was the world's richest colonial possession. Certain business men in France made huge profits.

"You'll get a colonial empire, Napoleon — all we'll get is profits."

It was these greedy men, hungry for more profits, who interested Napoleon in reenslaving Santo Domingo.

"Why, I conquered Italy with 40,000 troops!"

Santo Domingo CASUALTIES

Napoleon's inhumanity toward the negro patriots of Santo Domingo was no less than to his own French troops. Altogether, he sent over 40,000 fighting men, and none ever returned.

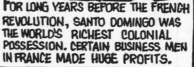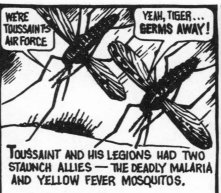

"We're Toussaint's air force"

"Yeah, Tiger... germs away!"

Toussaint and his legions had two staunch allies — the deadly malaria and yellow fever mosquitos.

"Don't cry, Pauline — I'll get you another husband.*"

The Santo Domingo affair also widowed Napoleon's favorite sister, Pauline. General Leclerc, her husband, was among the thousands who died of mosquito bites. *He did, too!

Toussaint was treacherously captured, while under a flag of truce, and died in a French prison. But the people of Santo Domingo, whom he led to liberation, are still free and independent...

"Toussaint really won..."

PLANS for SANTO DOMINGO / For LOUISIANA — TRASH

Also, Toussaint and his hard-biting mosquitos made scraps of paper of Napoleon's colonial plans, which included Louisiana...

MEANWHILE!

"Like Toussaint, I don't trust Napoleon."

The same year General Leclerc invaded Santo Domingo, Thomas Jefferson became President of the U.S.A. — and he was suspicious!

THERE'S *SOME* CONNECTION HERE...

LOUISIANA

USA

SANTO DOMINGO

PRESIDENT THOS. JEFFERSON SUSPECT-ED THAT NAPOLEON HAD SOMEHOW GOTTEN LOUISIANA AWAY FROM SPAIN.

YOU'LL SEE A LOT MORE OF ME.

ROBT. LIVINGSTON WAS APPOINTED MINISTER TO FRANCE, WITH SPECIAL INSTRUCTIONS TO *FIND OUT ABOUT LOUISIANA!*

LOUISIANA? FRANCE DOESN'T OWN ANY LOUISIANA. WHAT IS LOUISIANA, ANYWAY?

TALLEYRAND, WHO NEVER GAVE A STRAIGHT ANSWER IN HIS LIFE, REPLIED TO LIVINGSTON'S QUESTION...

JOHN BULL TOLD ME.

TREATY

RUFUS KING, U.S. MINISTER TO ENGLAND, LEARNED THAT NAPOLEON HAD LOUISIANA. TALLEYRAND LIED TO LIVINGSTON.

SHH-H! QUIET, MEN!

IT WAS ALSO LEARNED NAPOLEON HAD AN EXPEDITION UNDER WRAPS...TO SEND TO NEW ORLEANS, WHEN HE HAD SANTO DOMINGO SECURE.

IT WAS, THEREFORE, WITH KEEN INTEREST THAT PRESIDENT JEFFERSON FOLLOWED THE HEROIC RESIST-ANCE OF TOUSSAINT AND HIS FREE PEOPLE.

I CALLED IT HAITI..

THE INDIAN NAME FOR SANTO DOMINGO, WHERE TOUSSAINT MADE POSSIBLE THE U.S. PURCHASE OF LOUISIANA, IS **HAITI**... WHICH MEANS, "MOUNTAINS ALL OVER THE PLACE."

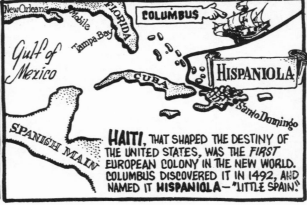

New Orleans

Mobile

FLORIDA

Tampa Bay

COLUMBUS

Gulf of Mexico

CUBA

HISPANIOLA

Santo Domingo

SPANISH MAIN

HAITI, THAT SHAPED THE DESTINY OF THE UNITED STATES, WAS THE *FIRST* EUROPEAN COLONY IN THE NEW WORLD. COLUMBUS DISCOVERED IT IN 1492, AND NAMED IT **HISPANIOLA** — "LITTLE SPAIN!"

PAPA WOULD LIKE THAT...

CITY LIMITS SANTO DOMINGO

SANTO DOMINGO, HISPANIOLA'S CAPITAL, WAS FOUNDED IN 1496, NAMED FOR COLUMBUS' DADDY. LATER, THIS BECAME THE <u>WHOLE</u> ISLAND'S NAME.

NO GOLD IN ALABAMA

...OR KANSAS.

DESOTO

CORONA

I WENT SWIMMING IN FLORIDA..

DE LEON

DE SOTO, CORONADO, PONCE DE LEON, AND ALL OTHER SPANISH CONQUISTADORES STARTED THEIR CAREERS FROM THE ISLAND VARIOUSLY CALLED HAITI, HISPANIOLA, AND SANTO DOMINGO.

ME... WORK! IT'LL KILL ME.

BUT WHATEVER NAME YOU CALL THIS BEAUTIFUL ISLAND, ITS HISTORY HAS BEEN VIOLENT. FIRST, THE SPANIARDS WORKED ALL THE INDIANS TO DEATH...

I'M LIVING IN A BRUTAL AGE.

THESE TREASURE-HUNTING SPANIARDS INTRODUCED SLAVERY TO THE NEW WORLD. AS THE INDIANS DIED OFF, THEY IMPORTED NEGROES FROM AFRICA. LATER, FRENCHMEN PAID FOR THIS INHUMANITY.

FIRST FRENCHMEN ON HAITI WERE BUCCANEERS! REFUGEES FROM SPANISH MIGHT ESCAPED TO THE HILLS. THEY LIVED ON BUCCAN, A KIND OF DRIED MEAT, AND SO WERE CALLED BUCCANEERS. AS THEIR NUMBER INCREASED, THEY BEGAN ATTACKING SHIPS..THUS, BUCCANEERS BECAME **PIRATES.**

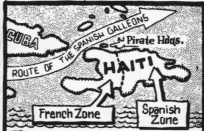

THEN, FRENCH BUCCANEERS SEIZED WESTERN HAITI. BY A TREATY IN 1697, THIS BECAME **ST. DOMINQUE** —OR FRENCH SANTO DOMINGO.

LIBERTY.. OR DEATH!

EXACTLY 100 YEARS LATER, TOUSSAINT LED THE SLAVES IN REVOLT. **536,000 SLAVES VS. 32,000 MASTERS!** AGAINST SLAVERY, NOT AGAINST FRANCE, WAS THIS REVOLUTION THAT TOUSSAINT LOUVERTURE LED.

I SHOULD HAVE LISTENED TO ADVICE — BUT DICTATORS NEVER DO.

NAPOLEON LIVED TO REGRET HIS MISTAKE IN HAITI. HE COULD HAVE RULED THROUGH TOUSSAINT — INSTEAD, LIVES OF COUNTLESS HAITIAN PATRIOTS AND OVER 40,000 FRENCHMEN WERE FORFEIT.

ONCE IN THE MISSISSIPPI VALLEY ... WE **WIN!**

THERE'S LITTLE DOUBT THAT NAPOLEON'S GRAND STRATEGY WAS (1) SUBDUE HAITI; THEN (2), MOVE OVER TO NEW ORLEANS — AND UP THE VALLEY OF THE MISSISSIPPI.

WELL, MIGHT UNCLE SAM STAND IN TRIBUTE TO TOUSSAINT LOUVERTURE AND HIS LEGIONS ... HAD THEY NOT BLED IN DEFENSE OF THEIR LIBERTY, AMERICANS IN THE OHIO VALLEY ALMOST SURELY WOULD HAVE DIED DEFENDING THEIRS.'

I WONDER IF WE'LL **EVER** HAVE PEACE?

OHIO VALLEY SETTLERS WERE GRAVELY CONCERNED OVER NAPOLEON'S HAITI ADVENTURE. "WE ARE NEXT ON THE LIST FOR FRENCH AGGRESSION," THEY FELT SURE.

THIS TIME, DETROIT AND US ARE ON THE SAME SIDE...

1802.. THE FRONTIER WAS EVER ON GUARD. LESS THAN 20 YEARS AGO NAVIGATION OF THEIR RIVER WAS THREATENED FROM THE **NORTH** — FROM THE BRITISH BASED AT FORT DETROIT.

BUT.. IN 1802, THE AMERICAN FLAG HAD FLOWN OVER FORT DETROIT FOR SIX YEARS, IN THREE MORE MICHIGAN TERRITORY **WOULD BE ORGANIZED... DETROIT,** THE **OLDEST BIG CITY WEST OF THE APPALACHIANS, WAS FOUNDED IN 1701.**

WHY... THEM DIRTY DUNS..

OCT. 16, 1802

—MORALES

NAPOLEON'S BEHIND THIS, I'LL BET IT.

BUT, IN 1802, TROUBLE FOR THE OHIO VALLEY CAME FROM AN UNEXPECTED SOURCE! NOT NAPOLEON, BUT **SPAIN!** WITHOUT EXPLANATION, THE SPANISH AT NEW ORLEANS CLOSED THE PORT TO AMERICANS.

GEE, BUT MY EARS **BURN!**

THE TOUGH BOATMEN WERE ENRAGED !! NOBODY HAS EVER BEEN MORE **EXPERTLY** CUSSED OUT THAN JUAN BUENAVENTURA MORALES, AFTER HE CORKED UP THE RIVER.

IT'LL BE INHUMAN —BUT WE'LL DO IT!

YEAH!

FURTHERMORE... THE BOATMEN THREATENED TO SEND DOWN **MIKE FINK** TO BEAT UP THE SPANISH ARMY!

MOST AMERICANS BLAMED NAPOLEON IN 1802, WHEN SPAIN CLOSED THE PORT OF NEW ORLEANS. AFTER ALL, SPAIN HAD GIVEN LOUISIANA BACK TO FRANCE IN 1800...

BUT FOR THOSE TWO YEARS AFTER THE RETROCESSION TREATY, WILY SPANISH MINISTERS PUT OFF DELIVERING THE POSSESSION OF LOUISIANA TO NAPOLEON.

THIS DELAY MADE NAPOLEON SO FURIOUS THAT HE REFUSED TO GIVE SPAIN HIS PICTURE, WHEN IT WAS OFFICIALLY REQUESTED IN APRIL, 1801.

EVEN THOUGH NAPOLEON'S PICTURE WAS REFUSED TO SPAIN, THAT NATION PUT A "FINISHING TOUCH" TO THE WAY AMERICANS PICTURED NAPOLEON.

NAPOLEON'S AGGRESSION IN HAITI, AND HIS PROPOSED EXPEDITION FOR LOUISIANA HAD MADE HIM UNPOPULAR ENOUGH IN THE U.S.A. CLOSING THE RIVER MADE HIM A POTENTIAL "MENACE"!

NINE DAYS AFTER SPAIN CLOSED THE PORT OF NEW ORLEANS, SHE FINALLY DELIVERED POSSESSION OF LOUISIANA TO NAPOLEON. ALAS, FOR NAPOLEON, IT WAS NOW TOO LATE.

IN OCT. 1802 – WHEN SPAIN PUT NAPOLEON IN POSSESSION OF LOUISIANA – THE FRENCH WERE LOSING SANTO DOMINGO. LECLERC DIED NOV. 2, AND SO DID FRENCH VICTORY.

GENERAL VICTOR'S EXPEDITION, WAITING IN HOLLAND TO SAIL FOR LOUISIANA, HAD BEEN STRIPPED OF SUPPLIES AND MEN TO REENFORCE LECLERC IN HAITI.

BEFORE VICTOR COULD BE REOUTFITTED, THE DUTCH WINTER HIT HIM. HIS EXPEDITION WAS ICE-BOUND, FROZEN STIFF UNTIL APRIL, 1803.

EVEN THOUGH NAPOLEON COULDN'T OCCUPY THE TERRITORIES HE HAD, HE WAS ALWAYS AFTER MORE. IN OCT. 1802, THE DUKE OF PARMA DIED, AND NAPOLEON SEIZED HIS ITALIAN DUCHY.

THIS DUKE, IT WILL BE REMEMBERED, WAS THE BROTHER OF THE QUEEN OF SPAIN. HE WAS TO GET MORE LAND IN ITALY, IN EXCHANGE FOR WHICH SPAIN WOULD LET FRANCE HAVE LOUISIANA.

BUT NAPOLEON GOT ANGRY WITH THE DUKE ABOUT SOMETHING. INSTEAD, HE MADE THE DUKE'S SON A KING OF A NEW KINGDOM HE THOUGHT UP IN ITALY. IT WAS NEXT DOOR TO THE DUKE'S PLACE ...

I'VE GOT A PROPOSITION FOR YOU, QUEENIE...

SPANISH ROYAL PALACE

WHEN THE DUKE OF PARMA DIED, NAPOLEON OFFERED TO GIVE THE DUKE'S ESTATE IN ITALY TO SPAIN, IN EXCHANGE FOR **FLORIDA**!

KING

HM-M... YOU MISSED YOUR CALLING, NAPOLEON — YOU OUGHTA BEEN A **HORSE-TRADER**.

PARMA for FLORIDA

NAPOLEON'S THINKING IN REAL ESTATE MATTERS IS VERY CONFUSING. HE HAD ACQUIRED LOUISIANA BY ADDING TO THE DUCHY OF PARMA... NOW HE PROPOSED ACQUIRING FLORIDA IN EXCHANGE FOR THE ORIGINAL DUCHY TO WHICH HE HAD ADDED!

MISS. ALA. GA.

LOUISIANA

FLORIDA

THE STORY OF **FLORIDA** ...THAT LOOKS LIKE A GREAT PISTOL LEVELED AT LOUISIANA, WILL SOON BE TOLD HERE.

IT WUZ LOADED!

GOLLY.. THIS IS JUST ABOUT **ALL** THE LAND IN OHIO AND ILLINOIS!

96,292 SQUARE MILES

THE OBSCURITY OF LOUISIANA'S BOUNDARIES WAS TO COST UNCLE SAM 96,292 SQUARE MILES AFTER THE PURCHASE. SPAIN CLAIMED THAT MUCH WASN'T IN IT...

GOT MY OWN FLAG, TOO.

W. FLA.

BLUE — WHITE STAR

WEST FLORIDA REVOLTED FROM SPAIN IN 1810, THEN JOINED THE U.S. AFTER 74 DAYS AS AN INDEPENDENT NATION.

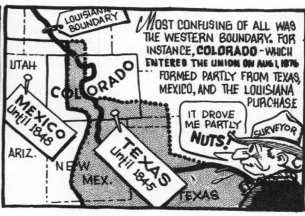

LOUISIANA BOUNDARY

UTAH

COLORADO

MEXICO Until 1848

ARIZ.

NEW MEX.

TEXAS Until 1845

TEXAS

MOST CONFUSING OF ALL WAS THE WESTERN BOUNDARY. FOR INSTANCE, **COLORADO** — WHICH ENTERED THE UNION ON AUG 1, 1876 FORMED PARTLY FROM TEXAS, MEXICO, AND THE LOUISIANA PURCHASE

IT DROVE ME PARTLY **NUTS**!

SURVEYOR

TREATY of AMIENS
Between France and England
Cease fire, Oct. 1, 1801
Treaty signed, March 28, 1802

SH-H!

UNDER COVER OF THIS TREATY, NAPOLEON HAD SOUGHT TO SET UP STRONG FRENCH COLONIES IN HAITI AND LOUISIANA...

TOUSSAINT

TIMETABLE

WE HAVE SEEN HOW HIS TIMETABLE WAS SO VIOLENTLY UPSET IN HAITI, AND HOW HIS LOUISIANA EXPEDITION WAS STALLED BY THE ICY DUTCH WINTER.

HEY!

ENGLAND SUSPECTED ALL THIS NAPOLEONIC ACTIVITY WAS IN PREPARATION FOR RENEWING THE FRANCO-BRITISH WAR... THE BRITISH LION WAS AROUSED!

SEA LION OF GREAT BRITAIN AT THE TIME OF NAPOLEON WAS.. **LORD NELSON**

HE BLOCKED NAPOLEON'S INVASION OF ENGLAND, AND BLOCKED HIS EXPEDITION TO LOUISIANA, TOO.

NELSON'S GENIUS FOR WAR AT SEA MATCHED NAPOLEON'S FOR WAR ON LAND. TOGETHER THEY MIGHT HAVE CONQUERED THE WORLD — BUT THEY PLAYED ON DIFFERENT TEAMS.

MY ONLY CONSOLATION IS — I MAKE NAPOLEON **SICKER**!

NELSON — THE WORLD'S GREATEST SEA FIGHTER — ALWAYS GOT SEASICK IN ROUGH WEATHER.

HEY! WHERE'S MY **xe** NAVY?

DOWN IN EGYPT NAPOLEON FIRST RAN INTO NELSON. THAT WAS WHEN NELSON RAN INTO HIS FLEET. THE BATTLE OF THE NILE IS CALLED THE WORLD'S MOST <u>COMPLETE</u> NAVAL VICTORY.

FOR THE NEXT FIVE YEARS, NELSON SUNK ABOUT EVERYTHING NAPOLEON FLOATED OUT AGAINST HIS FLEET. HIS SHIP WAS WELL-NAMED "VICTORY."

CAN I GET ANYTHING FOR YOU, NELSON – BESIDES NAPOLEON, I MEAN?

ONLY YOUR COMPANY, LADY HAMILTON.

FOR THE YEAR OF PEACE, 1802-03, NELSON RESTED IN ENGLAND. HE WAS 40 YEARS OLD, AND ALREADY HAD GIVEN HIS RIGHT ARM AND AND RIGHT EYE FOR HIS COUNTRY.

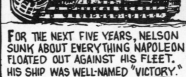

THEY MUST THINK SOME OF US AIM TO INVADE ENGLAND.

HOW'D THEY GUESS IT?

WITH REASON ENGLAND WAS SUSPICIOUS OF NAPOLEON'S 11,000 TROOPS IN HOLLAND, ALL SUPPOSED TO BE VICTOR'S EXPEDITIONARY FORCE FOR LOUISIANA — BUT VICTOR HAD TRANSPORTS FOR ONLY 3000 MEN! ENGLAND CLAMPED A BLOCKADE ON THE DUTCH COAST...

STAY HOME, NAPOLEON!

NELSON

COLONIES

THUS ENDED FOREVER NAPOLEON'S DREAM OF COLONIAL EMPIRE. NELSON'S BRITISH NAVY THAT STALLED HIS EGYPTIAN CAMPAIGN, AND TURNED HIS EFFORTS TO AMERICA, NOW DENIED HIM AMERICAN COLONIES, TOO.

I'LL SELL IT TO THOSE AMERICANS FIRST..

<u>AND</u>, LOUISIANA WAS A RIPE PLUM FOR NELSON TO PLUCK. NAPOLEON WAS DETERMINED TO PREVENT THIS...

B-BUT, MR. PRESIDENT... NATIONS DON'T <i>BUY</i> LAND. THEY <i>CONQUER</i> IT!

SUPPOSE WE TRY..

THE IDEA OF <i>PURCHASING</i> LOUISIANA APPEARS TO HAVE ORIGINATED WITH THOMAS JEFFERSON.

SEND LIVINGSTON $2,000,000 TO <i>BUY</i> NEW ORLEANS AND WEST FLORIDA.

WHEN IT WAS RUMORED THAT FRANCE OWNED LOUISIANA, HE SUMMONED HIS SECRETARY OF STATE, JAMES MADISON..

JUST SAY THE MAN WITH THE TWO MILLION IS BACK..

TALLEYRAND

SO.. AFTER SEPTEMBER OF 1801, ROBERT LIVINGSTON COMMENCED MONTHS AND MONTHS OF WEARY CAMPING ON THE DOORSTEPS OF FRENCH OFFICIALS.....

NOBODY WILL SAY YES..

$2 MILLION for NEW ORLEANS AND FLORIDA

..OR NO.

NOW, WE KNOW WHY LIVINGSTON GOT SO LITTLE SATISFACTION FOR SO LONG... NAPOLEON DIDN'T GET POSSESSION OF LOUISIANA FOR A YEAR AFTER THE TREATY OF SAN ILDEFONSO.

U.S.A.

WEST   Mobile   Biloxi

EAST FLORIDA

New Orleans

WHY, THE FIRST TWO CAPITALS OF LOUISIANA WERE IN FLORIDA!

IT NEVER OCCURRED TO JEFFERSON THAT WEST FLORIDA WAS NOT RETURNED TO NAPOLEON WITH LOUISIANA. NAPOLEON WAS MAKING EVERY EFFORT TO GET IT, THOUGH.

LOUISIANA

U.S.A.

IF I DON'T GET IT, THE ENGLISH WILL..

FLORIDA

QUICK TO RECOGNIZE "THE PISTOL POINTING AT LOUISIANA", NAPOLEON SOUGHT FLORIDA BECAUSE LOUISIANA WAS INDEFENSIBLE WITHOUT IT.

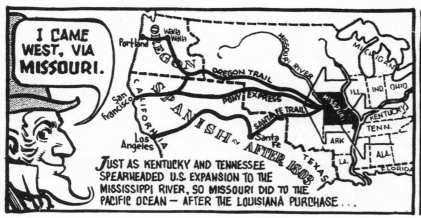

I CAME WEST, VIA MISSOURI.

JUST AS KENTUCKY AND TENNESSEE SPEARHEADED U.S. EXPANSION TO THE MISSISSIPPI RIVER, SO MISSOURI DID TO THE PACIFIC OCEAN — AFTER THE LOUISIANA PURCHASE...

AUG. 10, 1821, IS THE BIRTHDAY OF MISSOURI STATE. ALL THE FAMED TRAILS TO THE PACIFIC STARTED OUT FROM WESTERN MISSOURI.

ALL I GOT IS LEAD NICKELS. THAT'S GOOD AS GOLD, SON.

LEAD MINES STIMULATED MISSOURI SETTLEMENT, AND IN COLONIAL MISSOURI **LEAD WAS MONEY.**

SPECIAL SALE! 800 Acres... $42 -Terms To Suit- MISSOURI

RAPID SETTLEMENT OF THE OHIO VALLEY ALARMED SPAIN. LAND IN SPANISH MISSOURI WAS OFFERED TO AMERICANS REAL CHEAP. MANY MOVED OVER, BUT THEY DIDN'T BECOME SPANISH SUBJECTS.

HEY, PA — WE WUZ ROBBED! WE PAID 5¢ MISSOURI NEWS U.S. PAYS ONLY 4¢ AN ACRE

SEVEN YEARS AFTER THIS, THE U.S. BOUGHT ALL OF MISSOURI FOR ONE CENT AN ACRE LESS THAN SPAIN'S BARGAIN PRICE — BOUGHT MISSOURI, AND 839,456 SQUARE MILES BESIDES!

LEAD MINE — JOPLIN, MO.

IN MISSOURI, WHERE ONCE LEAD WAS MONEY, LEAD IS STILL *WORTH MONEY.* IN FACT, IN ONE YEAR-1950-MISSOURI PRODUCED LEAD VALUED AT $36,349,020 — OR, OVER TWICE THE COST OF THE LOUISIANA PURCHASE!

Capitol Building Jefferson City.

JEFFERSON CITY IS THE CAPITAL OF MISSOURI, AND AN ENDURING MONUMENT TO THOMAS JEFFERSON, WHOSE DIPLOMACY IN 1803 WAS PRIZE-WINNING...

WAR WITH ENGLAND NO FLORIDA DEATH OF LECLERC VICTOR ICE-BOUND

THE PRIZE, OF COURSE, WAS LOUISIANA. IN 1803, EVERYTHING WAS GOING RIGHT FOR JEFFERSON — AND EVERYTHING WAS GOING WRONG FOR NAPOLEON.

JEFFERSON'S FIRST TASK IN 1803 WAS TO PREVENT WAR. THE OHIO VALLEY WAS ON THE VERGE OF STARTING ONE...

THEY LOVED ME ON THE FRONTIER.

JAN. 1803: JEFFERSON NAMED **JAMES MONROE** AS *EXTRA*-SPECIAL MINISTER TO FRANCE... WAR TALK IN THE OHIO VALLEY SUBSIDED IMMEDIATELY.

SCRAM!

WITH THE COUNTRY BEHIND HIM, JEFFERSON COULD NOW PURSUE HIS MEASURES *SHORT OF WAR* TO GET NEW ORLEANS AWAY FROM NAPOLEON.

MONROE DOCTRINE I WASN'T BIG ENOUGH TO SWING THIS UNTIL AFTER 1803.

MONROE LATER BECAME 5th U.S. PRESIDENT. HISTORIANS NOW AGREE HIS FAMOUS "MONROE DOCTRINE" COULD *NEVER* HAVE HAPPENED, IF THE LOUISIANA PURCHASE HAD NOT HAPPENED *FIRST*.

DOESN'T JEFFERSON TRUST ME..

$2,000,000 FOR N.O. AND FLA.

MONROE IS COMING

MEANWHILE, IN FAR-AWAY PARIS, LIVINGSTON TOOK A DIM VIEW OF HAVING ANOTHER MAN IN HIS OFFICE.

I SHOULD OF STOOD IN BED!

...AND WHILE MONROE WAS SAILING FOR PARIS, PETER CLEMENT LAUSSAT WAS SAILING FOR NEW ORLEANS — TO TAKE OVER LOUISIANA FOR NAPOLEON.

THIS IS GOING TO BE THE MOST UNPRIVATE BATH IN HISTORY.

BUT—

TOMORROW IS SATURDAY, AND NAPOLEON HAS TO TAKE HIS BATH — ALSO, MAKE UP HIS MIND ABOUT LOUISIANA...

CHASE

I THOUGHT THIS WOULD BE OFF THE RECORD.

NAPOLEON'S FIRST RECORDED STATEMENT OF HIS DECISION TO SELL LOUISIANA TO THE U.S. WAS MADE FROM HIS BATHTUB ON APRIL 7, 1803.

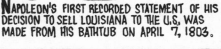
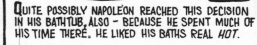

I'M IN HOT WATER IN LOUISIANA, TOO.

QUITE POSSIBLY NAPOLEON REACHED THIS DECISION IN HIS BATHTUB, ALSO — BECAUSE HE SPENT MUCH OF HIS TIME THERE. HE LIKED HIS BATHS REAL HOT.

THEY SAY HE WASHES EVERY DAY!

UGH!

SOME FRENCHMEN MUTTERED THAT NAPOLEON BATHED TOO MUCH... CLEANLINESS WAS STILL A NEW-FANGLED IDEA IN 1803.

CHASE

I'M SELLING LOUISIANA!!

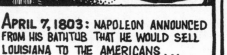

APRIL 7, 1803: NAPOLEON ANNOUNCED FROM HIS BATHTUB THAT HE WOULD SELL LOUISIANA TO THE AMERICANS...

I WAS THERE!

LUCIEN WAS NAPOLEON'S POLITICIAN BROTHER, AND HE WROTE UP NAPOLEON'S UN-PRIVATE BATH IN HIS MEMOIRS.

BROTHER JOE WAS IN THE BATHROOM, TOO.

LUCIEN WAS MINISTER TO SPAIN, WHEN THE TREATY RETURNING LOUISIANA TO FRANCE WAS SIGNED. THE KING OF SPAIN GAVE LUCIEN $225,000 IN DIAMONDS AS A PRESENT FOR SIGNING.

CHASE

JOSEPH WAS NAPOLEON'S BIG BROTHER. HE HAD NEGOTIATED FOR THAT LAND IN ITALY WHICH NAPOLEON GAVE TO SPAIN IN EXCHANGE FOR LOUISIANA.

CHASE

I WONDER.. WILL I HAVE TO GIVE BACK MY DIAMONDS?

BOTH LUCIEN AND JOE HAD WORKED HARD TO GET LOUISIANA FOR NAPOLEON, AND THEY WERE SHOCKED TO HEAR HIM SAY HE WAS SELLING IT.

I HAD TO GIVE THESE BACK...

CROWN OF SPAIN

CROWN OF NAPLES

UNLIKE LUCIEN, JOE DIDN'T GET DIAMONDS FOR HIS CONFERENCE WORK. BUT NAPOLEON DID MAKE HIM A KING — IN FACT, HE MADE JOE TWO KINGS!

ALTOGETHER, NAPOLEON HAD FOUR BROTHERS, AND HE MADE KINGS OF THREE OF THEM.

LUCIEN PREFERRED TO REMAIN A POLITICIAN. BESIDES, HE NEVER FORGAVE NAPOLEON FOR SELLING LOUISIANA.

NAPOLEON ALSO MADE HIS SISTER CAROLINE A QUEEN, AND SISTER ELISE A DUCHESS.

BUT PAULINE, HIS KID SISTER, PREFERRED TO REMAIN THE QUEEN OF HEARTS. SHE WAS THE FLIRT OF THE FAMILY.

BUT BROTHER JOE WAS NOT YET A KING THAT DAY IN APRIL, 1803. HE WAS PROVOKED WITH NAPOLEON, THREATENING TO REPORT HIM TO THE CHAMBER OF DEPUTIES (FRENCH CONGRESS.)

THIS MADE NAPOLEON FURIOUS, AND HE SPLASHED HIS BATH WATER ALL OVER BROTHER JOE.

JOE LEFT TO GO DRY OUT, AND LUCIEN RESUMED THE DISCUSSION WITH NAPOLEON. "SELLING LOUISIANA IS UNCONSTITUTIONAL", SAID LUCIEN. THEREUPON, NAPOLEON STARTED THROWING THINGS, AND BROTHER LUCIEN ALSO TOOK HIS DEPARTURE...

FOLLOWING NAPOLEON'S HOT BATH, AND HIS HOT ARGUMENTS WITH BROTHERS JOE AND LUCIEN, HE SUMMONED HIS FOREIGN MINISTER...

FOR MONTHS LIVINGSTON HAD BEEN PROPOSITIONING TALLEYRAND TO SELL *ONE TOWN* IN LOUISIANA. TALLEYRAND WOULD NEVER EVEN ANSWER HIM.

SO, ON APRIL 11, 1803..
LIVINGSTON WAS DUMBFOUNDED!!

SELLING LOUISIANA IS A GOOD DEAL! I'LL CREATE A NAVAL RIVAL FOR ENGLAND!

BESIDES, I CAN'T DEFEND THE COLONY... THAT NELSON SINKS EVERYTHING...

ALSO, I'LL SHOW SPAIN — WOULDN'T GIVE ME FLORIDA, WOULD THEY!

MAYBE THE U.S. WILL LIKE ME BETTER, TOO.

BUT... *NOBODY* LIKES TALLEYRAND. I'LL ASSIGN BARBE-MARBOIS TO DICKER WITH LIVINGSTON. ALL THE AMERICANS LIKE *HIM!*

Next

THE MAN WHO SOLD LOUISIANA..

I WAS THE MOST INDESTRUCTIBLE POLITICIAN OF MY TIME...

François Barbé-Marbois WAS A FRENCH OFFICE-HOLDER WHO SURVIVED *THREE* REVOLUTIONS, THE RISE AND FALL OF NAPOLEON, AND SCARCELY MISSED A DAY AT THE OFFICE IN 66 YEARS OF CIVIL SERVICE!

IT'S A GOOD POLICY, BUT WILL IT WORK?

OH, WE HAVE TO LEAVE *THAT* TO MARBOIS.

MARBOIS NEVER HEADED A GOVERNMENT, BUT HE IS ONE OF THE GREAT ADMINISTRATORS OF MODERN TIMES. HOWEVER, THE WORLD REMEMBERS MARBOIS BEST AS... "THE MAN WHO SOLD LOUISIANA"!

I HOPE YOU WIN YOUR REVOLUTION, SIR. OTHERWISE I LOSE MY JOB.

BARBÉ-MARBOIS' FIRST IMPORTANT JOB WAS FRENCH REPRESENTATIVE TO THE UNITED STATES AT THE TIME OF THE REVOLUTIONARY WAR. HE KNEW WASHINGTON, AND *ALL* THE FOUNDING FATHERS.

YOU'RE MY *FAVORITE* AMERICAN MISS MOORE

MARBOIS GREW TO LOVE THE AMERICAN PEOPLE, ESPECIALLY THE DAUGHTER OF WILLIAM MOORE OF PENNSYLVANIA. SHE BECAME HIS JUNE BRIDE IN 1784.

THIS WAS MY *MOST* DANGEROUS REVOLUTION!

AFTER SIX YEARS IN THE U.S., MARBOIS WAS PROMOTED INTENDANT OF FRENCH SANTO DOMINGO. HE WAS THERE WHEN TOUSSAINT LED HIS PEOPLE IN REVOLT, BUT HE SURVIVED THIS REVOLUTION, TOO.

EXCUSE *ME*!

HEADS

ALREADY A VETERAN OF TWO REVOLUTIONS, MARBOIS RETURNED TO FRANCE TO BE ENDANGERED BY THE REIGN OF TERROR OF THE FRENCH REVOLUTION. HE SURVIVED!

B-MARBOIS OFFICE-IN-EXILE

HERE, I'M SURVIVING YELLOW FEVER

EFFICIENT MARBOIS DIDN'T THINK MUCH OF THE FRENCH DIRECTORY GOVERNMENT. FOR THIS HE WAS HUSTLED OFF TO DEVIL'S ISLAND AS A POLITICAL EXILE FOR TWO YEARS.

THAT DOG-GONE NAPOLEON HAS BEEN HERE *AGAIN*!

FRENCH CASH

WHEN NAPOLEON CAME TO POWER, MARBOIS RETURNED FROM EXILE TO BECOME HIS TREASURER—NO EASY JOB FOR A SPENDTHRIFT LIKE NAPOLEON.

I'VE DECIDED TO SELL LOUISIANA— ANY ARGUMENTS?

PASSPORTS TO DEVIL'S ISLAND

A FEW DAYS AFTER NAPOLEON'S BATHTUB ARGUMENTS WITH HIS BROTHERS, HE CALLED A MEETING OF SOME OF HIS OFFICE-HOLDERS TO "ASK THEIR OPINION" OF HIS PLAN TO SELL LOUISIANA. MARBOIS WAS THERE.

TELL LIVINGSTON I WANT TEN MILLION DOLLARS.

FOLLOWING THIS MEETING WITH HIS "ADVISORS", THE JOB OF SELLING LOUISIANA WAS ENTRUSTED TO MARBOIS.

TEN MILLION, INDEED! I'LL GET TWENTY!

DEED TO LOUISIANA

MARBOIS WAS A FRIEND OF THE UNITED STATES, BUT HARDLY A BENEFACTOR... HE *DOUBLED* THE PRICE NAPOLEON WANTED FOR LOUISIANA!

SHREWD AND SMART WAS BARBÉ-MARBOIS, WHO HAD SURVIVED THREE REVOLUTIONS. IN 1803, HE WAS WORKING FOR NAPOLEON, AND HE KNEW THE VALUE OF LOUISIANA BETTER THAN HIS BOSS — SO HE DOUBLED THE PRICE.

NAPOLEON WAS SMART, TOO, IN APPOINTING MARBOIS TO SELL LOUISIANA. HE STILL ENJOYED FRIENDLY RELATIONS WITH THE U.S.

BESIDES, MARBOIS' VERY BEST AMERICAN FRIEND WAS JAMES MONROE, WHO WAS THOS. JEFFERSON'S SECRET WEAPON!

(You'll see - tomorrow.)

THOMAS JEFFERSON SAW TO IT THAT NAPOLEON FOUND OUT THAT MONROE'S "SECRET" MISSION WAS, (1) BUY NEW ORLEANS AND FLORIDA, OR . . .

(2) MOVE OVER TO LONDON AND MAKE A BRITISH-AMERICAN ALLIANCE, WHEREBY THE U.S. WOULD GET NEW ORLEANS

THIS IS WHY NAPOLEON RUSHED HIS TREASURER, BARBÉ-MARBOIS, INTO SELLING LOUISIANA. IF HE DID NOT SELL IT, HE WOULD LOSE IT — AND LOSE FACE, TOO.

THE PURCHASE LIFTED THE UNITED STATES TO GREATNESS AMONG NATIONS, AND—WITHIN 150 YEARS - TO THE LONELY ROLE OF WORLD LEADERSHIP. UNCLE SAM, AS HE PEERS AHEAD INTO COURSES UNCHARTED, MAY FIND NEW STRENGTH FOR HIS TASK. BECAUSE, SO LONG AS HIS MOTIVES ARE UNSELFISH, HE IS NOT ALONE. JEFFERSON WASN'T!

WE HAVE SEEN HOW THE BEGINNING OF OHIO VALLEY SETTLEMENT AND NAPOLEON COINCIDED EXACTLY. ONE GREW UP TO DEMAND PURCHASE OF LOUISIANA, THE OTHER SO GREW THAT HE HAD TO SELL IT.

IN THE ACCOUNTS OF "THE GREAT PLANNER", THE HARDSHIPS AND SUFFERING OF OHIO VALLEY PIONEERS, AND TOUSSAINT LOUVERTURE'S HAITIANS ARE PART OF THE PRICE PAID FOR THE LOUISIANA PURCHASE

IN APRIL, 1803, IN PARIS, LIVINGSTON BOUGHT LOUISIANA. AT THIS SAME TIME, IN WASHINGTON, JEFFERSON AUTHORIZED THE LEWIS AND CLARK EXPEDITION. THEN, JEFFERSON HAD NO IDEA LOUISIANA HAD BEEN PURCHASED — BUT THE "GREAT PLANNER" KNEW IT

JAMES MONROE ARRIVED IN PARIS APRIL 12, 1803. LIVINGSTON HAD HIM OVER FOR DINNER THAT NIGHT...

WHILE LIVINGSTON AND MONROE WERE SIPPING AFTER-DINNER COFFEE, BARBÉ-MARBOIS WAS SEEN OUTSIDE. HE WAS ACTUALLY PEDDLING LOUISIANA AT LIVINGSTON'S DOOR!

MARBOIS WAS INVITED IN FOR COFFEE, AND A DATE WAS MADE FOR NEXT DAY

LIVINGSTON'S DATE WITH MARBOIS ON APRIL 13 WAS BEFORE 11 A.M. HE MADE MONROE STAY IN BED, AND WENT ALONE.

AT THIS MEETING LIVINGSTON REALIZED THAT LOUISIANA WAS IN THE BAG! BUT HE COMPLAINED ABOUT THE PRICE; AFTER ALL, $20 MILLION WAS TWO YEARS' REVENUE OF THE UNITED STATES GOVERNMENT. BESIDES, THE U.S. NATIONAL DEBT IN 1803 WAS $7,300,000.

A LESSER MAN THAN LIVINGSTON MIGHT HAVE RESULTED IN NO LOUISIANA PURCHASE IN 1803. HE WAS CONVINCED THAT THE LOUISIANA WILDERNESS WAS A GOOD BUY, AND ROBT. LIVINGSTON HAD THE COURAGE OF HIS CONVICTIONS...

LIVINGSTON ALSO HAD TO GET MONROE TO STRING ALONG WITH HIM. MONROE HAD VERY SPECIFIC INSTRUCTIONS: BUY NEW ORLEANS AND FLORIDA, FOR NOT MORE THAN $10 MILLION — AND NOTHING ELSE!

THEN COMMENCED THREE WEEKS OF HAGGLING OVER THE PRICE OF LOUISIANA...

AFTER A LONG SESSION ON APRIL 29, LIVINGSTON AND MARBOIS REACHED AGREEMENT. THE PRICE OF LOUISIANA WAS 80,000,000 FRANCS ($15,000,000)

MONROE AGREED, TOO. HE WAS SICK, AND SPENT THE WHOLE OF THIS MEETING LYING ON A COUCH. HISTORIANS DON'T SAY WHAT AILED MONROE ON APRIL 29, 1803.

BUT THE THOUGHT OF WHAT CONGRESS MIGHT DO WHEN IT LEARNED WHAT HAPPENED THAT DAY IN PARIS WAS ENOUGH TO MAKE MONROE ILL— HIM, AND LIVINGSTON TOO!

150 YEARS AGO UNCLE SAM BOUGHT LOUISIANA WITH DOLLARS.

NAPOLEON, HOWEVER, RECEIVED PAYMENT IN FRANCS.

I WAS ALMOST TWO BITS' WORTH! YEAH.

IN 1803, FIVE AND ONE-THIRD FRENCH FRANCS EQUALED ONE AMERICAN DOLLAR.

I NEED A LOAN!

TO PAY NAPOLEON 80 MILLION FRANCS, UNCLE SAM NEEDED 15 MILLION DOLLARS — MORE THAN HE TOOK IN IN TWO YEARS.

I MADE A NEAT PROFIT.

U.S. PUBLIC LANDS $1.25 PER ACRE (OR 6 FRANCS)

LOUISIANA

IN 1803, WHEN UNCLE SAM BORROWED 15 MILLION DOLLARS TO PAY NAPOLEON 80 MILLION FRANCS, HE GOT TEN ACRES FOR EACH FRANC.

HI, FRANC! BON JOUR, M'SIEUR.

IN 150 YEARS, VALUE OF THE FRENCH FRANC HAS DROPPED TO 400 FOR ONE DOLLAR, ON THE FREE MARKET. AND LOUISIANA PURCHASE LAND HAS RISEN '

HECK! I CAN ONLY PUT ENOUGH OF THAT IN CORN TO RAISE ABOUT 550 HOGS.

FARM FOR SALE! SAME PRICE LA. PURCHASE (IN FRANCS)

FOR INSTANCE... THE BEST IOWA AND ILLINOIS CORN LAND SOLD FOR $600 AN ACRE RECENTLY. TODAY, 60 MILLION FRANCS BUYS ONLY 333 ACRES!

IT'S FOR MY UNCLE SAM — HE WANTS TO BUY A PIECE OF PROPERTY.

THE BANK

IN APRIL, 1803, ROBERT LIVINGSTON NOT ONLY HAD TO DECIDE WHETHER UNCLE SAM OUGHT TO BUY LOUISIANA —— HE ALSO HAD TO ARRANGE A LOAN TO PAY FOR THE PURCHASE!

THIS IS MY FRIEND, ALEX — HE'S GOT MONEY!

LIVINGSTON INTRODUCED ALEXANDER BARING TO MARBOIS. BARING REPRESENTED THE TWO BIGGEST BANKS IN EUROPE, BOTH ENGLISH-OWNED.

I FIGHT SOLDIERS, NOT BANKERS!

ALTHOUGH NAPOLEON WAS GOING TO WAR WITH ENGLAND THE NEXT MONTH, HE HAD NO OBJECTION TO ENGLISH BANKERS IN APRIL, 1803.

I GOT LOUISIANA! I GOT $9,750,000 —NET.

NOT THE LEAST OF THE AMAZING THINGS ABOUT THE LOUISIANA PURCHASE STORY WAS HOW THE DEAL WAS FINANCED.

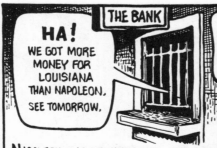

HA! WE GOT MORE MONEY FOR LOUISIANA THAN NAPOLEON. SEE TOMORROW.

THE BANK

NAPOLEON —AS WE HAVE SEEN — HAD TO SELL LOUISIANA. OR THE ENGLISH NAVY WOULD TAKE IT.... INSTEAD, THE ENGLISH BANKERS "TOOK" NAPOLEON!

HISTORIANS SAY I DID THIS OUTTA FRIENDSHIP FOR THE U.S.

BAM! BAM!

JOHN BULL MADE NO OBJECTION TO ENGLISHMEN LOANING AMERICANS MONEY TO DAY TO NAPOLEON, EVEN THOUGH THIS ENGLISH MONEY WAS TO BE USED BY NAPOLEON TO MAKE WAR ON ENGLISHMEN.

THE ACT OF SALE THAT TRANSFERRED LOUISIANA TO THE UNITED STATES IN 1803 WAS A **TREATY**. IT IS NOTEWORTHY THAT FRANCO-AMERICAN RELATIONS, HAVE BEEN CORDIAL EVER SINCE THAT DAY.

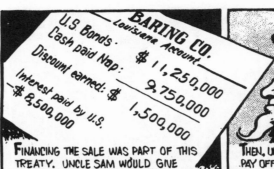

BARING CO.
Louisiana Account

U.S. Bonds: $ 11,250,000
Cash paid Nap: 9,750,000
Discount earned: $ 1,500,000
Interest paid by U.S. $ 8,500,000

FINANCING THE SALE WAS PART OF THIS TREATY. UNCLE SAM WOULD GIVE NAPOLEON BONDS, WHICH BARING WOULD CASH FOR NAPOLEON IMMEDIATELY.

THE BANK GOT $250,000 *MORE* THAN NAPOLEON— BUT I GOT LOUISIANA!

THEN, UNCLE SAM HAD EIGHTEEN YEARS TO PAY OFF HIS LOAN TO BARING, WITH INTEREST AT 6% PER YEAR. ALL THIS LIVINGSTON AND MONROE ARRANGED FOR UNCLE SAM.

WHEN DO WE REACH NEW YORK?

OH, WITH A SWELL TAIL WIND LIKE THIS.. NEXT MONTH.

LIVINGSTON AND MONROE *HAD* TO ARRANGE EVERYTHING FOR THE LOUISIANA PURCHASE. IN 1803, IT TOOK *MONTHS* TO TRANSACT TRANS-ATLANTIC BUSINESS. THERE WASN'T TIME!

YOU'RE A SUPER MINISTER, MR. LIVINGSTON — BUT *I'D* HAVE TO SEND YOU TO DEVIL'S ISLAND.

DICTATOR

CERTAINLY NOBODY BUT THE REPRESENTATIVE OF A GOVERNMENT OF FREE PEOPLE COULD ASSUME THE RESPONSIBILITIES LIVINGSTON DID IN 1803. A DICTATOR WOULD BE JEALOUS OF SUCH AN ENTERPRISING MINISTER, AND FEAR HIM AS A RIVAL,

DAMAGE CLAIMS

LIVINGSTON MIGHT HAVE BEEN PRESIDENT — EXCEPT FOR *ME*!

AS PART OF THE PRICE OF LOUISIANA, THE U.S. GOVERNMENT ASSUMED DAMAGE CLAIMS OF U.S. CITIZENS AGAINST FRANCE...THESE DAMAGE CLAIMS DAMAGED LIVINGSTON.

Robt. Livingston

HE CANNOT BE GIVEN ENOUGH CREDIT FOR THE PURCHASE... HIS MONTHS OF PERSISTENT EFFORT WERE SURELY WHAT FINALLY DID INFLUENCE NAPOLEON TO SELL. AND MONROE ARRIVED TOO LATE TO DO OTHER THAN STRING ALONG WITH LIVINGSTON'S POLICY.

YEAH.. TWO STRIKES ON ME.

BUT, IN 1801, LIVINGSTON WENT TO PARIS WITH **TWO** IMPORTANT ASSIGNMENTS.

HECK... NOBODY TO FIGHT NOW, 'CEPT INJUNS AN' PIRATES.

SECURING FREE USE OF THE RIVER AND THE PORT OF NEW ORLEANS WAS ONE,... THE LOUISIANA PURCHASE ACCOMPLISHED THIS.

I'M A BLINKING BILL COLLECTOR!

FRENCH GOVT.

LIVINGSTON'S OTHER ASSIGNMENT IN PARIS WAS TO GET FRANCE TO PAY THE DAMAGE CLAIMS DUE AMERICAN CITIZENS...

I DIDN'T SAY *WHEN* WE'D PAY!

FRENCH GOVT.

DURING THAT UNDECLARED NAVAL WAR MANY U.S. MERCHANTS SUFFERED LOSSES. BY THE TREATY, IN 1800, THAT ENDED THE HOSTILITIES, FRANCE PROMISED TO PAY.

THE WEST

HUH, *YOU*!

THE EAST

THUS LIVINGSTON REPRESENTED **TWO** SECTIONS: THE OHIO VALLEY FRONTIER WANTED NEW ORLEANS, AND EASTERN SEABOARD EXPORTERS WANTED THEIR CLAIMS MONEY.

LOUISIANA PURCHASE

ALL I WANTED WAS A PORT. OHIO VALLEY

FOR THE OHIO VALLEY FRONTIER LIVINGSTON SOUGHT ONLY NEW ORLEANS, OR ANOTHER GULF PORT.

THIS ISN'T SECTIONAL! NOW, IT CONCERNS ALL THE UNITED STATES. PROPOSITION TO BUY ALL LOUISIANA

BUT WHEN HE WAS OFFERED THE WHOLE LOUISIANA TERRITORY THAT DOUBLED THE SIZE OF THE U.S... THEN, DAMAGE CLAIMS ASSUMED A SECONDARY IMPORTANCE.

..BUT I COULDN'T QUEER THE WHOLE LOUISIANA PURCHASE!!

WE WUZ ROBBED!

EVEN SO, A SETTLEMENT OF THESE CLAIMS BECAME PART OF THE PURCHASE TREATY. THE U.S. WITHHELD $3,750,000 OF THE $15,000,000 PRICE PAID AS SETTLEMENT OF THE CLAIMS. LATER, IT WAS CHARGED THIS WASN'T ENOUGH!

NO CONTRACT WAS EVER NEGOTIATED WITH MORE MUTUAL GOOD WILL, THAN THE LOUISIANA PURCHASE TREATY. ALL THE PRINCIPALS WERE FRIENDS, ALL TRUSTED EACH OTHER IMPLICITLY.

IT'S GREEK TO ME — BUT WHERE DO I SIGN?

FOR EXAMPLE, FIRST DRAFT OF THE TREATY WAS IN FRENCH, WHICH LIVINGSTON COULDN'T READ. BUT LIVINGSTON SIGNED IT ANYWAY!

WEREN'T YOU ELIZABETH MOORE, MRS. MARBOIS?

WHY, YES— AND **YOU** WERE ANNE BINGHAM!

NOT ONLY WERE LIVINGSTON, MONROE, MARBOIS AND BARING ALL FRIENDS; BUT BOTH MARBOIS' WIFE AND ANNE BARING, WIFE OF THE ENGLISH BANKER, WERE PENNSYLVANIA GIRLS!

BY THE LOUISIANA PURCHASE, THE U.S. CERTAINLY BENEFITED MOST OF ALL.

I PAID THE BRITISH BACK — WITH LEAD!

BUT NAPOLEON GOT $9,750,000 IN CASH MONEY.

—BUT IT TOOK ME 18 YEARS.

ALEXANDER BARING GOT $10,000,000 IN DISCOUNTS AND INTEREST.

CASH, TOO! WITH APPRECIATION-NAP.

MARBOIS GOT $34,129 —A GIFT FROM NAPOLEON.

YOU'RE ELECTED, MONROE.

MONROE GOT TO BE PRESIDENT OF THE UNITED STATES.

HOW'S BUSINESS, LIVINGSTON?

EXCELLENT... BUT I WAS FORCED INTO IT.

BUT LIVINGSTON GOT NOTHING! BLAMED FOR THE TOO SMALL SETTLEMENT OF THE DAMAGE CLAIMS, 'HE NEVER HELD A PUBLIC OFFICE AGAIN.

LIVINGSTON WAS BOSS — HE TOOK THE RAP...

POLITICALLY UNINJURED BY THE CLAIMS SETTLEMENT, **JAMES MONROE**, WENT ON TO BECOME 5th. U.S. PRESIDENT.

AT THE 100th. ANNIVERSARY OF THE PURCHASE, **THEODORE ROOSEVELT**, 26th. PRESIDENT, MADE A SPEECH AT THE ST. LOUIS WORLD FAIR.

I GREW UP IN KANSAS, A LOUISIANA PURCHASE STATE

DWIGHT D. EISENHOWER THE 34th. PRESIDENT SPOKE IN NEW ORLEANS AT FESTIVITIES MARKING THE 150th. ANNIVERSARY OF THE PURCHASE.

LOUISIANA PURCHASE

57

A FEW YEARS AFTER THE PURCHASE, "THE PISTOL POINTING AT LOUISIANA" EXPLODED.

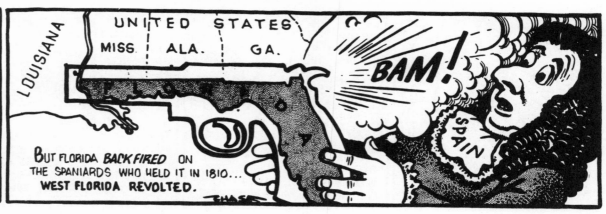
BUT FLORIDA *BACK FIRED* ON THE SPANIARDS WHO HELD IT IN 1810... WEST FLORIDA REVOLTED.

LIVINGSTON WAS PARTLY DEAF AND UNABLE TO TALK FRENCH, BUT HE WASN'T LEFT-HANDED... INSTRUCTED TO BUY THE LEFT BANK OF THE RIVER, HE BOUGHT THE **RIGHT** BANK

EXCEPTING NEW ORLEANS, **ALL** THE PURCHASE WAS ON THE RIGHT SIDE OF THE RIVER. LIVINGSTON WORRIED ABOUT WHAT THE FOLKS BACK HOME MIGHT SAY

SO HE CHECKED UP, AND FOUND THAT HISTORICALLY LOUISIANA HAD *ALWAYS* INCLUDED THE GULF COAST BEYOND MOBILE. JEFFERSON AGREED, BUT SPAIN RAISED AN AWFUL SQUAWK!

BY 1810, FLORIDA HAD ALREADY BEEN SPANISH FOR 280 YEARS, AND ENGLISH FOR 20 — BUT MOST OF THE INHABITANTS WERE ENGLISH-AMERICANS.

WHEN THESE AMERICANS IN WEST FLORIDA HEARD THEY WEREN'T INCLUDED IN THE LOUISIANA PURCHASE, THEY DID WHAT JEFFERSON HAD FEARED THE OHIO VALLEY MIGHT DO A FEW YEARS EARLIER. **THEY REVOLTED!**

THE REPUBLIC OF WEST FLORIDA DECLARED INDEPENDENCE ON SEPT. 23, 1810. IT WAS ANNEXED TO THE U.S. 74 DAYS LATER.

THE BRITISH WERE GREAT FOR DRAWING LINES. THEY DIVIDED FLORIDA INTO **EAST** AND **WEST** AT THE APALACHICOLA RIVER.

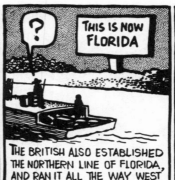
THE BRITISH ALSO ESTABLISHED THE NORTHERN LINE OF FLORIDA, AND RAN IT ALL THE WAY WEST TO THE MISSISSIPPI RIVER.

BY THE REVOLT OF 1810, THE U.S. ACQUIRED MOST OF WEST FLORIDA. THE BALANCE — THE PRESENT STATE OF FLORIDA — WAS PURCHASED FROM SPAIN FEB. 22, 1819.

TAXING THE PEOPLE WAS CONTRARY TO JEFFERSON'S DEMOCRATIC IDEAS. ALL INTERNAL TAXES WERE CUT OUT.

IMAGINE WAKING UP SOME MORNING, AND FINDING NO TAXES!

YOU JUST DID, PA!

THE PEOPLE LOVED HIM FOR ENDING FEDERAL TAXATION; AND JEFFERSON WHO SOUGHT TO BE A LEADER IN NAME ONLY, BECAME A *POWERFUL* PRESIDENT.

HOORAY FOR TOM!

HE'S ALL RIGHT!

HOUSE OF REPRESENTATIVES

HEY, SENATOR - RUN GET ME A SANDWICH!

YES, MR. CONGRESSMAN, SIR.

THEN, CONGRESS INCREASED JEFFERSON'S POWER. IN 1803, THE SENATE WAS JUST A DEBATING SOCIETY. MORE IMPORTANT WAS THE HOUSE, WHERE MEMBERS ALWAYS VOTED JUST LIKE THE FOLKS BACK HOME WANTED —— AND ALL THE FOLKS WANTED TO DO *WHATEVER* TOM JEFFERSON SAID!

U.S. REVENUE 1801

Customs.. $9,500,000
Sale of land & Postage stamps.. 450,000
Taxes... 650,000
Total... $10,600,000

AFTER WE CUT OUT TAXES, WE'LL HAVE $9,950,000.

ALBERT GALLATIN, WHOSE HOME WAS ON THE FRONTIER NEAR PITTSBURGH, WAS SECRETARY OF THE TREASURY. HE COULD *REALLY* ECONOMIZE!!

THIS WILL LEAVE $2,650,000 TO RUN THE COUNTRY, MR. PRESIDENT.

THAT'S *PLENTY*, GALLATIN.

JEFFERSON WAS DETERMINED TO PAY OFF THE NATIONAL DEBT. GALLATIN FIGURED IT COULD BE ALL PAID IN SIXTEEN YEARS, BY PAYING $7,300,000 ON THE DEBT *EVERY YEAR*.

ITS THIS WAY, GENTLEMEN — *BOTH* ENGLAND AND NAPOLEON WANT OUR FRIENDSHIP. *THEY'LL* FIGHT OUR BATTLES.

GALLATIN'S ECONOMY PROGRAM JUST BEFORE THE LOUISIANA PURCHASE ALLOWED ONLY $1,600,000 FOR NATIONAL DEFENSE. BUT JEFFERSON WASN'T WORRIED.

ARMY... UGH!

HOWEVER, THE $930,000 FOR SUPPORT OF THE ARMY DIDN'T KEEP THE INDIAN MUCH IN AWE...

*@!!

U.S.S. TUB

THE U.S. NAVY, AT THIS TIME, GOT ALONG ON $670,000.

I WAS PAID $6 A DAY, TOO.

7TH CONGRESS

WASHINGTON, D.C.- 150 YEARS AGO - WAS LESS IMPRESSIVE THAN ANY STATE CAPITAL, AND THE CONGRESS MORE LIKE ANY STATE LEGISLATURE...

HEY SENATOR! HITCH UP MY TEAM — WE'RE GOING HOME.

YESSIR, MR. CONGRESSMAN.

THE 7TH CONGRESS ADJOURNED ON MARCH 4, 1803. JEFFERSON HAD NO MEASURES — AND THERE SURELY WASN'T ANY *MONEY* TO APPROPRIATE FOR ANYTHING.

I'LL CHANGE THINGS!

LOUISIANA PURCHASE

Thos. Jefferson

THIS WAS THE STATE OF THE UNION WHEN NEWS OF THE LOUISIANA PURCHASE ARRIVED.

At the time of the Louisiana Purchase, Uncle Sam was in SHORT PANTS.

THAT'S ME, ALL OVER!

Uncle Sam is the cartoonist's symbol for national unity—the people of ALL the states.

THIS MEANS ME!

THE PEOPLE

JEFFERSON'S REPUBLICAN-DEMOCRATS

National unity came of age in Jefferson's administration. So did Uncle Sam—and so did long pants. You'll see...

Like cold water in the morning, FEDERALISTS awakened the new nation to a need for UNITY...

CONSTITUTION

I'LL PROTECT YOU, SON—I'M A FEDERALIST.

First federalists were men who championed the constitution. Later, federalists were those who believed the people unfit to govern. "WE'LL GOVERN FOR 'EM," said they.

DEMOCRACY HAS NEVER WORKED BEFORE.

HA! BUT I FOOLED ALEX!

AMERICAN PEOPLE

Able Alexander Hamilton emerged as head of the Federalist PARTY. Hamilton feared democracy, which means "rule by the people."

Thus, TWO parties began. Jefferson was leader of the Democrats.

BLOODY-REPUBLICAN!

STUFFY FEDERALIST!

When U.S. party politics began, a man's dress was a matter of political conviction! Federalists dressed like conservative Englishmen, Democrats like radical French.

WOMEN weren't in politics then. ALL women followed the Paris style, with high-high waist and narrow skirt.

D-DID YOU SEE THAT FRENCH LADY?

YES, AND I FEEL LIKE A PEEPING TOM!

BUT—English and American women never dared peel down to the few clothes, which were the ultra in Parisian fashions of these times.

Jefferson, leader of the Democrats, didn't wear long pants, but his workingman's shoes, with floppy laces irked Federalists as much.

Politically-wise Jefferson affected ill-fitting, mussed, hand-me-down-looking clothes. The people loved him for it!

TOM'S JUST PLAIN FOLKS LIKE US!

HE'S SETTING WASHINGTON FASHION BACK 25 YEARS.

YEAH—BACK TO THE INDIANS!

Thus did Jefferson taunt the well-groomed Federalists, suspected by many of favoring a monarchy for Americans—with a "royal" court.

...THE MOST WONDERFUL WORK EVER STRUCK OFF AT A GIVEN TIME BY THE BRAIN AND PURPOSE OF MAN.

WILLIAM GLADSTONE, ENGLISH STATESMAN, HAS PAID THE U.S. CONSTITUTION ITS FINEST TRIBUTE.

THAT HAMILTON READ ME BETWEEN MY LINES

THE CONSTITUTION, WHICH UNITED THE PEOPLE IN 1787, HAD DIVIDED THEM INTO TWO PARTIES BY 1800...

MY GOODNESS!

BUT THIS WAS A WHOLESOME DIFFERENCE OF OPINION. JEFFERSON INSISTED THE CONSTITUTION BE FOLLOWED TO THE LETTER—

HOORAY! WE'VE GOT NEW ORLEANS!

..AND A LOT MORE!

ON JULY 14, 1803, WHEN JEFFERSON RECEIVED THE TREATY WHICH WAS THE LOUISIANA PURCHASE, HE WAS ELATED!

MY GOSH.. IT'S UNCONSTITUTIONAL!

THEN, THE PRESIDENT'S DEMOCRATIC SENSIBILITIES WERE SHOCKED!

HOW DO YOU SPELL PRECEDENT?

IMMEDIATELY, HE SCRIBBLED OUT AN AMENDMENT — TO MAKE THE LOUISIANA PURCHASE LAWFUL!

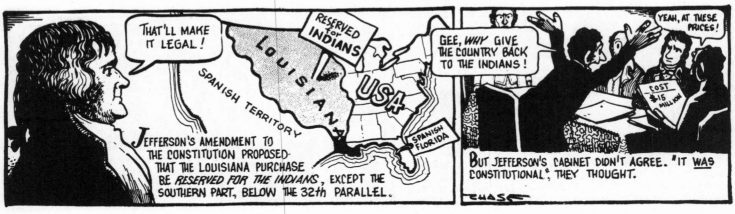

THAT'LL MAKE IT LEGAL!

RESERVED FOR INDIANS

JEFFERSON'S AMENDMENT TO THE CONSTITUTION PROPOSED THAT THE LOUISIANA PURCHASE BE RESERVED FOR THE INDIANS, EXCEPT THE SOUTHERN PART, BELOW THE 32th PARALLEL.

GEE, WHY GIVE THE COUNTRY BACK TO THE INDIANS!

YEAH, AT THESE PRICES!

COST $15 MILLION

BUT JEFFERSON'S CABINET DIDN'T AGREE. "IT WAS CONSTITUTIONAL", THEY THOUGHT.

WE MUST ASK THE PEOPLE...IT SAYS HERE

NOT NECESSARY!

NO!

WHILE JEFFERSON AND HIS CABINET DEBATED THE CONSTITUTIONALITY OF THE LOUISIANA PURCHASE, CONGRESS WAS ENROUTE TO WASHINGTON.

WE'LL BE THERE IN 5 DAYS NOW, SENATORS.

WASHINGTON 200 MILES

IN CONCORD COACHES, MEMBERS OF CONGRESS COULD HASTEN TO WASHINGTON. AVERAGE SPEED WAS 4 MILES AN HOUR. MEMBERS WERE ALLOWED $6 FOR EVERY 20 MILES OF TRAVEL.

LOUISIANA PURCHASE

STAGECOACH SCHEDULE to WASHINGTON

Philadelphia.....4 days
New York.........6 days
Boston...........9 days
Pittsburgh....10 days
Points South....Horseback Only

ONE HUNDRED AND FIFTY YEARS AGO ALL CONGRESSMEN WERE A LONG WAY FROM HOME.

..AND THIS IS ONLY IF IT DON'T RAIN.

I HAD TO GET TO OHIO..

IN 1802, THE SAME BILL THAT PROPOSED STATEHOOD FOR OHIO ALSO PROVIDED FOR THE FIRST U.S. HIGHWAY. IT COST ALMOST AS MUCH AS THE LOUISIANA PURCHASE TO BUILD.

BUT... I DON'T SEE OUR NEW CAPITOL.

COURSE NOT, SILLY—YOU'RE STANDING BEHIND THAT TREE.

NEW MEMBERS OF THE 8th CONGRESS, ARRIVING IN WASHINGTON IN 1803 TO OK THE LOUISIANA PURCHASE, HAD DIFFICULTY *FINDING* THE U.S. CAPITOL...

HI, SENATOR!

HI, CONGRESSMAN!

IN 1803, WHEN THE EIGHTH CONGRESS MET TO CONSIDER THE LOUISIANA PURCHASE, THE CAPITOL AT WASHINGTON LOOKED LIKE THIS.

AH! YOU'RE THE NEW SENATOR FROM OHIO?

NO, I'M THE THE NEW PLASTERER FROM PITTSBURGH.

THE U.S. CAPITOL WAS UNDER CONSTRUCTION 150 YEARS AGO, AND SO WAS THE NATION ITSELF. THE U.S. AND ITS CAPITOL HAVE GROWN BIG TOGETHER.

IN 1803 – HOUSE OF REPRESENTATIVES, NOW STATUARY HALL.

OLD SENATE. ONLY THESE TWO SECTIONS OF CAPITOL EXISTED IN 1803.

THE NATION'S CAPITOL IS MANY TIMES LARGER THAN BUILDINGS IN WHICH CONGRESS CONVENED IN 1803 TO VOTE FOR THE LOUISIANA PURCHASE. THE *NATION* IS MANY TIMES LARGER TOO!

GEE! NAPOLEON MIGHT CHANGE HIS MIND!

JUST BEFORE CONGRESS MET IN OCTOBER, 1803, JEFFERSON RECEIVED ALARMING NEWS FROM ROBERT LIVINGSTON IN PARIS...

WAIT'LL THE FEDERALISTS HEAR ABOUT THIS!

CONSTITUTION

THE SHELF

NEXT WEEK!

IN ORDER TO SAVE THE PURCHASE, JEFFERSON INSTRUCTED ADMINISTRATION LEADERS IN CONGRESS NOT TO *MENTION* THE CONSTITUTION. "HURRY AND RATIFY THE LOUISIANA TREATY," SAID JEFFERSON.

DON'T YOU WANT TO SIT, AND HEAR THE PRESIDENT'S MESSAGE?

SIT! I'VE BEEN SITTING ON A HORSE ALL THE WAY FROM CHARLESTON.

ON OCT 17, 1803, THE 8th CONGRESS RECEIVED THE PRESIDENT'S MESSAGE ON LOUISIANA. MEMBERS HAD TRAVELED WEARY DAYS AND WEEKS TO BE IN ATTENDANCE ON OCT. 17, 1803.

IN 1953, PRESIDENT EISENHOWER TRAVELED FROM KANSAS CITY TO NEW ORLEANS IN ONE MORNING. IN 1803 THIS WAS A JOURNEY OF MANY WEEKS.

LAND SAKES!

CONSTITUTION

THE LOUISIANA PURCHASE BREEZED THROUGH CONGRESS IN TWO WEEKS, BUT THE CONSTITUTION HAS NEVER BEEN QUITE THE SAME SINCE...

LOUISIANA PURCHASE

WE WOULD *NEVER* HARM THE CONSTITUTION.. / IT'S OUR LIFE INSURANCE!

STATES RIGHTERS

JEFFERSON AND HIS VIRGINIA COLLEAGUES WERE ARDENT STATES RIGHTERS. THEY WANTED LOUISIANA — AND THEY ALSO WANTED TO BE CONSTITUTIONAL.

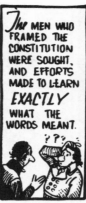

The MEN WHO FRAMED THE CONSTITUTION WERE SOUGHT, AND EFFORTS MADE TO LEARN *EXACTLY* WHAT THE WORDS MEANT.

GEE! I *MUST* HAVE MEANT THE LOUISIANA PURCHASE WAS OK!

GOUVERNEUR MORRIS, IN CHARGE OF THE *PHRASEOLOGY* OF THE WRITTEN CONSTITUTION IN 1787, WAS ASKED IF THE PURCHASE WAS CONSTITUTIONAL . . .

I CAN BE BENT, MAYBE – BUT NOT BROKEN!

CONSTITUTION / THE FUTURE

THE LOUISIANA PURCHASE WAS THE GREAT PRECEDENT. IT LIFTED THE CONSTITUTION FROM "DEATHLESS PROSE" TO LIVING LAW.

WHILE CONGRESS DEBATED THE LOUISIANA PURCHASE, THE FRENCH AMBASSADOR RUSHED A FRENCH NAVAL OFFICER OFF TO NEW ORLEANS, WITH OFFICIAL AUTHORITY TO TRANSFER LOUISIANA FROM SPAIN TO FRANCE. HE LEFT WASHINGTON OCT. 13...

RUSH! / New Orleans 1,135 MILES

I CALCULATE HE TRAVELED 1 3/100 MILES PER HOUR.

ON NOV. 25 – 43 DAYS LATER! – THE RUSH ORDERS REACHED NEW ORLEANS. HISTORIANS STILL WONDER WHAT ROUTE THIS NAVAL OFFICER TOOK ??

HUH!

M. LAUSSAT RECEIVED THIS MESSAGE. HE WAS THE NO. 1 VICTIM OF THE LOUISIANA PURCHASE –

ONLY KNOWN PICTURE OF **PETER LAUSSAT** SHOWS A SAD-FACED, FAT LITTLE FRENCH BUREAUCRAT HE ARRIVED IN NEW ORLEANS MARCH 24, 1803.

THIS JOB MAKES ME SAD — AND FAT.

LAUSSAT AND GENERAL VICTOR WERE TO GOVERN LOUISIANA FOR NAPOLEON. LAUSSAT WAITED AND WAITED FOR VICTOR'S ARRIVAL, AND WHILE HE WAITED HE ATE AND ATE — AT DINNER PARTIES GIVEN IN HIS HONOR.

THE BRITISH NAVY, AND THE DUTCH WINTER DETAINED ME... *PERMANENTLY.*

Gen'l. Victor

...NOT EVEN A CIRCULAR, MAYBE? / ...NOT EVEN

NO COLONIAL ADMINISTRATOR EVER GOT LESS MAIL THAN LAUSSAT IN NEW ORLEANS. NAPOLEON FORGOT ABOUT HIM.

BUT, FELLOWS.. LOOK!

DURING THIS SPRING OF 1803, LAUSSAT TRIED TO IMPRESS THE SPANISH AUTHORITIES WITH HIS FUTURE IMPORTANCE — AFTER GENERAL VICTOR'S ARRIVAL. HE WAS IGNORED.

? / NO! / NO!

OHIO

ON MAY 17, 1803 THE SPANIARDS REOPENED THE PORT OF NEW ORLEANS TO THE OHIO RIVER BOATMEN. LAUSSAT BLEW HIS TOP ABOUT THIS.

CHASE

CHASE

COLONIAL PREFECT LAUSSAT, THE FORGOTTEN MAN OF 1803, LEARNED NAPOLEON HAD DECLARED WAR ON ENGLAND IN AN OLD JAMAICA NEWSPAPER.

AND NAPOLEON'S GOVERNMENT FORGOT TO INFORM ITS OFFICIAL IN NEW ORLEANS THAT LOUISIANA HAD BEEN SOLD OUT FROM UNDER HIM.

FIRST RUMORS OF THE LOUISIANA PURCHASE REACHED NEW ORLEANS FROM WASHINGTON DURING THE SUMMER OF 1803. FURIOUSLY, LAUSSAT BRANDED THEM *LIES!*

ON AUGUST 10, 1803 LAUSSAT LEARNED THAT THE RUMORS WERE TRUE. *LOUISIANA HAD BEEN SOLD!* THE FRENCH GOVERNMENT FINALLY WROTE HIM A LETTER..

THE PURCHASE WAS THE GREATEST DISAPPOINTMENT OF LAUSSAT'S CAREER. FOR FIVE MONTHS HE HAD BEEN PROCLAIMING THE WONDERFUL FUTURE FOR LOUISIANA UNDER FRENCH RULE. AND NOW, THIS WAS NOT TO BE

LAUSSAT WAS ALSO INFORMED, AT THIS TIME, THAT *HE* WAS TO RECEIVE POSSESSION OF LOUISIANA FROM SPAIN, AND THEN TRANSFER IT TO THE U.S.A.

THE LETTER THAT TOLD LAUSSAT OF THE PURCHASE, ALERTED HIM TO BE ON THE LOOKOUT FOR THE OFFICIAL ORDERS BEING *RUSHED* BY SPECIAL COURIER.

THESE RUSH ORDERS, COMMISSIONING LAUSSAT TO RECEIVE LOUISIANA FROM SPAIN, CAME BY THAT NAVAL OFFICER WHO MADE THE SLOWEST RUSH TRIP BETWEEN WASHINGTON AND NEW ORLEANS ON RECORD—*43 DAYS!*

MEANWHILE JEFFERSON HAD BEEN ORGANIZING A U.S. COMMISSION TO ACCEPT DELIVERY OF LOUISIANA.

ON OCT. 31, 1803, ALL LEGISLATION ENABLING THE U.S. TO TAKE POSSESSION OF LOUISIANA WAS PASSED AND SIGNED BY THOMAS JEFFERSON.

ALSO, ON OCT. 31, 1803 GENERAL WILKINSON AND GOVERNOR CLAIBORNE WERE COMMISSIONED TO GO TAKE POSSESSION OF THE NEW TERRITORY.

BUT, SINCE JULY 17, 1803, JEFFERSON HAD BEEN CORRESPONDING WITH GOV. CLAIBORNE OF MISSISSIPPI ABOUT THE PURCHASE. AND THE PRESIDENT USED THE **U.S. MAIL!**

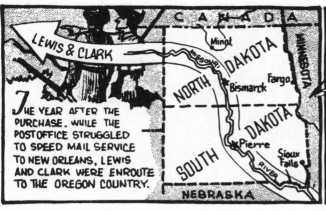

THE YEAR AFTER THE PURCHASE, WHILE THE POST OFFICE STRUGGLED TO SPEED MAIL SERVICE TO NEW ORLEANS, LEWIS AND CLARK WERE ENROUTE TO THE OREGON COUNTRY.

NORTH AND SOUTH DAKOTA ARE REAL TWINS! THEY ENTERED THE UNION ON THE SAME DAY, NOV. 2, 1889. BUT 84 YEARS BEFORE THEY BECAME STATES, THE KEELBOAT OF LEWIS AND CLARK WAS POLED UP THE MISSOURI TO THE SITE OF BISMARCK, N.D. BEYOND BISMARCK, THE EXPEDITION PUSHED ON IN CANOES. THE PARTY NUMBERED 32, AND ONE OF THEM WAS A WOMAN.

ME SHOW 'EM

SACAGAWEA, THE BIRD WOMAN, GUIDED LEWIS AND CLARK WESTWARD.

CHASE

AFTER 1803, POSTAL ROUTES REACHED OUT TO LINK LOUISIANA WITH THE U.S. NATIONAL CAPITAL. OFTEN THESE ROUTES WERE HARDLY ROADS AT ALL, BUT SERVICE WAS MAINTAINED WITH NEW ORLEANS (1500 MILES AWAY), AND ST. LOUIS (975 MILES DISTANT).

POSTAL ROUTES WEST

CHASE

GIDEON GRANGER WAS U.S. POSTMASTER GENERAL AT THE TIME OF THE LOUISIANA PURCHASE. IT WAS HIS JOB TO BIND THE NEW PROVINCE TO THE UNITED STATES WITH POSTAL ROUTES. MR. GIDEON'S SALARY WAS $3000, AND HE HAD SEVEN CLERKS.

THE DEPARTMENT

MIND, NOW— I CONSIDER ANY CONTRACT OVER $100 A MONTH AS EXTRAVAGANT.

A NEW POSTAL ROUTE WAS AWARDED TO A CONTRACTOR WHO BID LOWEST. THEN, THE CONTRACTOR HIRED THE RIDERS. DURING 13 YEARS IN OFFICE, GRANGER DOUBLED THE POSTAL ROUTE MILEAGE.

BEFORE THE PURCHASE TREATY WAS RATIFIED, GRANGER HAD A MAIL ROUTE TO NEW ORLEANS IN OPERATION.

CHASE

THE APPALACHIANS MADE DIRECT POSTAL ROUTES TO THE WEST DIFFICULT. EARLY ROUTES EITHER WENT INTO THE OHIO VALLEY NEAR PITTSBURGH, OR THROUGH THE CUMBERLAND GAP TO TENNESSEE.

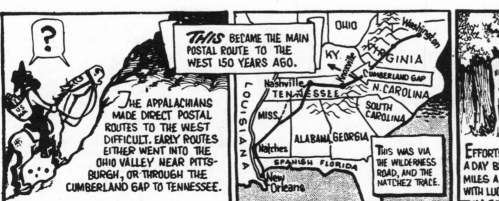

THIS BECAME THE MAIN POSTAL ROUTE TO THE WEST 150 YEARS AGO.

THIS WAS VIA THE WILDERNESS ROAD, AND THE NATCHEZ TRACE.

EFFORTS WERE MADE TO CARRY THE MAIL 100 MILES A DAY BETWEEN WASHINGTON AND NASHVILLE, AND 50 MILES A DAY FROM NASHVILLE TO NEW ORLEANS. WITH LUCK, THE TRIP COULD BE MADE IN A MONTH.

CHASE

WELL NOW, SI — I DID HAVE YE A LETTER. BUT IT WAS SO FULL OF BAD NEWS THET I T'ROWED IT IN THE CRICK.

IN 1803, FRONTIER POST RIDERS WERE CHOSEN FOR ENDURANCE AND EXPERIENCE IN THE WILDERNESS. SOME WERE NOSEY FELLOWS WHO READ THE MAIL!

I JES HOPE EVERYBODY WROTE WITH WATERPROOF INK.

WITH NO BRIDGES AND LITTLE PROTECTION FROM RAIN, KEEPING MAIL DRY WAS A BIG POSTOFFICE PROBLEM ON THE WILD FRONTIER POST ROUTES.

HOW ABOUT WRITING YOUR CONGRESSMAN? I NEED THE BUSINESS.

POSTAL RATES
40 MILES - 8¢
200 MILES - 17¢
OVER 500 - 35¢
NO CREDIT - DON'T ASK.

JUNCTION POSTOFFISE

IN 1803, POSTMASTERS IN TOWNS WERE PAID A PERCENTAGE OF POSTAL BUSINESS THEY HANDLED — BUT THESE COMMISSIONS COULD NOT EXCEED $1800 A YEAR.

WITH AMAZING SPEED AND EFFICIENCY, POSTAL ROUTES TIED THE NEW LOUISIANA TERRITORY INTO THE ECONOMIC AND COMMERCIAL LIFE OF THE U.S. — AND THE POSTOFFICE GREW GREAT PERFORMING THIS GREAT SERVICE.

POST OFFICE

POSTOFFICES IN THE U.S. INCREASED FROM 75 IN 1790, TO 903 IN 1800 — AND, AFTER THE PURCHASE, TO 1,558 POSTOFFICES.

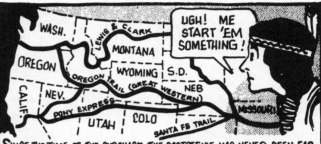

UGH! ME START 'EM SOMETHING!

WASH. / OREGON / CALIF. / NEV. / UTAH / LEWIS & CLARK / MONTANA / WYOMING / S.D. / NEB / COLO / MISSOURI / OREGON TRAIL (GREAT WESTERN) / PONY EXPRESS / SANTA FE TRAIL

SINCE THE TIME OF THE PURCHASE, THE POSTOFFICE HAS NEVER BEEN FAR BEHIND FRONTIER SETTLEMENT. LESS THAN 20 YEARS AFTER THE LEWIS AND CLARK EXPEDITION, THE 4,536 MILES LONG "GREAT WESTERN ROUTE" WAS PROPOSED - TO THE PACIFIC!

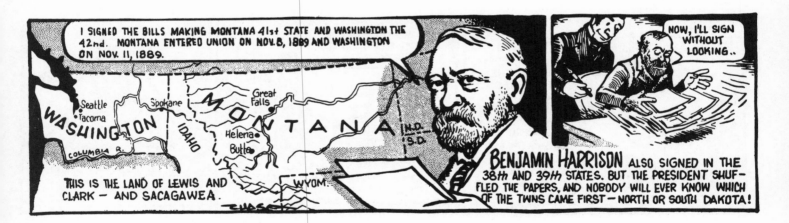

I SIGNED THE BILLS MAKING MONTANA 41st STATE AND WASHINGTON THE 42nd. MONTANA ENTERED UNION ON NOV. 8, 1889 AND WASHINGTON ON NOV. 11, 1889.

Seattle / Tacoma / Spokane / WASHINGTON / IDAHO / Great Falls / MONTANA / Helena / Butte / COLUMBIA R. / WYOM. / N.D. S.D.

THIS IS THE LAND OF LEWIS AND CLARK — AND SACAGAWEA.

NOW, I'LL SIGN WITHOUT LOOKING..

BENJAMIN HARRISON ALSO SIGNED IN THE 38th AND 39th STATES. BUT THE PRESIDENT SHUFFLED THE PAPERS, AND NOBODY WILL EVER KNOW WHICH OF THE TWINS CAME FIRST — NORTH OR SOUTH DAKOTA!

LEWIS / CLARK

AS GOOD A BARGAIN, AS THE $15 MILLION VOTED FOR LOUISIANA, WAS THE $2,500 CONGRESS VOTED TO FINANCE THE EXPEDITION OF **LEWIS and CLARK!**

ME CALLED SA-CA-GA-WEA

ME, POMPY.

THEY ESTABLISHED THE NORTHWEST LIMITS OF THE LOUISIANA PURCHASE, AND THE U.S. CLAIM TO THE OREGON TERRITORY.

BUT WITHOUT AN INDIAN GIRL TO SHOW THE WAY, LEWIS AND CLARK COULD NOT HAVE DONE THIS!

SACAGAWEA WAS BORN IN THE MOUNTAINS OF WEST MONTANA. SHE REMEMBERED THE PASSES AND TRAILS, AND SHOWED LEWIS AND CLARK THE WAY.

IT'S THE PASS!

GEE! WE NEVER WOULD HAVE FOUND IT!

TO NORTH DAKOTA

WHEN AGE 12, SHE HAD BEEN TAKEN CAPTIVE BY TRIBAL ENEMIES, AND CARRIED FAR DOWN THE MISSOURI. SACAGAWEA WAS A SLAVE.

BUT WHY DOES HE BRING HIS SQUAW—AND KID?

NO BABY SITTER, HE SAYS.

ME POMPY.

A FEW YEARS LATER, SHE WAS BOUGHT BY A FRENCH COUREUR DE BOIS, WHO MARRIED HER. LEWIS AND CLARK HIRED THIS FRENCHMAN AS INTERPRETER, AND HIS YOUNG INDIAN WIFE AND LITTLE BABY ACCOMPANIED HIM.

NON SPEEK ENGLAIS — ONLY COUNT IT!

#! $

CHARBONNEAU, SACAGAWEA'S FRENCH HUSBAND TURNED OUT TO BE A WORTHLESS FELLOW, AND PANICKY IN TIME OF DANGER. HOWEVER, HE WAS PAID $500.

HORSES ASK HIM.

LES CHEVAUX.

BXOMJR

SMKLRP

UGH!

CHARBONNEAU SPOKE ONLY FRENCH, AND DIALECTS OF THE PLAINS INDIANS. HIS WIFE SAVVIED THE TALK OF THE PLAINS INDIANS, AND ALSO MOUNTAIN INDIAN TALK. SO, WHEN LEWIS HAD TO ASK THE MOUNTAIN INDIANS FOR HORSES, *THREE* TRANSLATIONS WERE REQUIRED.

THEY CHANGED MY NAME TO SNAKE, AND MY GIRL'S NAME TO MUD! NO WONDER I SHOT MYSELF OCT. 11, 1809.

LEWIS

BEYOND THE MOUNTAINS, LEWIS AND CLARK NAMED FORKS OF THE COLUMBIA FOR EACH OTHER. CLARK RIVER REMAINED, BUT THE LEWIS IS NOW CALLED SNAKE RIVER.

WE WERE *ALL* THERE!

RIVERS AND LANDMARKS WERE NAMED FOR *EVERY* MEMBER OF THE LEWIS & CLARK EXPEDITION. MANY STILL REMAIN IN MONTANA. ALSO, RIVERS NAMED FOR JEFFERSON AND HIS CABINET ARE STILL SO CALLED.

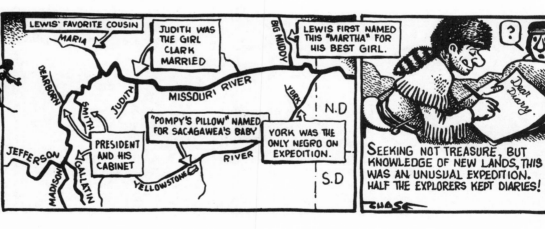

LEWIS' FAVORITE COUSIN

MARIA

JUDITH WAS THE GIRL CLARK MARRIED

BIG MUDDY

LEWIS FIRST NAMED THIS "MARTHA" FOR HIS BEST GIRL.

DEARBORN

SMITH

JUDITH

MISSOURI RIVER

YORK

N.D

JEFFERSON

MADISON

GALLATIN

PRESIDENT AND HIS CABINET

"POMPY'S PILLOW" NAMED FOR SACAGAWEA'S BABY

YORK WAS THE ONLY NEGRO ON EXPEDITION.

RIVER

YELLOWSTONE

S.D

?

Dear Diary

SEEKING NOT TREASURE, BUT KNOWLEDGE OF NEW LANDS, THIS WAS AN UNUSUAL EXPEDITION. HALF THE EXPLORERS KEPT DIARIES!

SERGEANT ORDWAY ONLY WROTE 100,000 WORDS.

HUH, WHAT CAN YOU EXPECT—A *SERGEANT*!

BY CAPT. LEWIS

BY CAPT. CLARK

MERIWETHER LEWIS AND WILLIAM CLARK, THE LEADERS OF THE EXPEDITION, ALSO LED IN THE SIZE OF THEIR DIARIES... 900,000 WORDS, OF WHICH ABOUT 197,425 WERE MISSPELLED.

x!*

DICTIONARY

MD

HISTORIANS HIGHLY PRAISE THIS EXPEDITION. EVERYTHING WAS SO WELL PLANNED. LEWIS AND CLARK ONLY FORGOT TO BRING TWO THINGS —A DOCTOR, AND A DICTIONARY.

GULP! I'LL WRITE YOU IN ALL CAPITALS!

BESIDES DISCOVERING NEW LANDS, LEWIS AND CLARK ALSO DISCOVERED A NEW WAY TO USE CAPITALS — FOR SMALL ANIMALS THEY USED SMALL LETTERS, BIG ONES THE WROTE IN CAPITALS.

WHEN THE DIARIES WERE PRINTED, THE EDITORS DID NOT CHANGE THE INGENIOUS SPELLING. EDITORS, LIKE LOUISIANA, HAVE CHANGED SINCE 1803

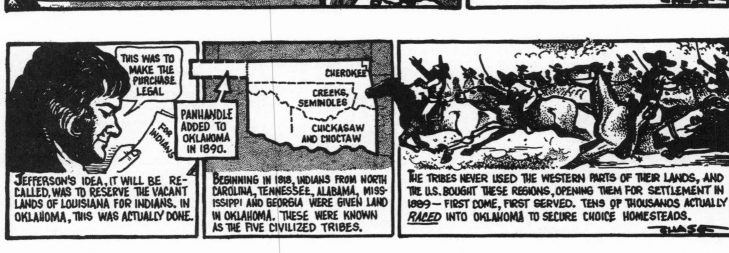

THE LOUISIANA PROVINCE WHICH THE U.S. BOUGHT FROM NAPOLEON WAS SUPPOSED TO BE THE SAME IN SIZE AS THE LOUISIANA FRANCE HAD GIVEN TO SPAIN BACK IN 1762

THE JOKER WAS THAT *NOBODY* KNEW THAT SIZE! THERE SIMPLY WAS NO WESTERN BOUNDARY!

THE U.S. CLAIMED AS FAR WEST AS THE RIO GRANDE, AND THE PACIFIC — OR, JUST ABOUT *EVERYTHING* EXCEPT THE PRESENT STATES OF CALIFORNIA, NEVADA, UTAH, AND ARIZONA. SPAIN SUGGESTED THE MISSISSIPPI MIGHT BE THE WEST BOUNDARY!

IT WAS IN 1816 THAT THE U.S. PRESSED ITS CLAIM THAT THE WEST BOUNDARY OF LOUISIANA WAS THE RIO GRANDE. SPAIN REJECTED THIS CLAIM.

IN FACT, AT THIS TIME, SPAIN OFFERED TO CEDE ALL FLORIDA TO THE U.S. — IF THE U.S. WOULD DROP CLAIM TO *ALL* LOUISIANA, EXCEPT NEW ORLEANS.

BUT THE LEWIS AND CLARK EXPEDITION BOLSTERED U.S CLAIM TO THE FAR WESTERN LANDS. AND SO DID THE EXPEDITION OF LIEUTENANT **PIKE**

15 U.S. SOLDIERS "CUT DOWN 14 LOGS AND PUT UP A BREAST WORK, 5 FEET HIGH ON 3 SIDES."* THIS WAS THE FIRST STRUCTURE ERECTED IN COLORADO'S SECOND CITY.

* from Lieut. Pike's Journal.

FOR FIVE MONTHS, LIEUT. PIKE AND HIS 15 SOLDIERS HAD BEEN ENROUTE FROM ST. LOUIS. GEN. WILKINSON HAD SENT THE LIEUTENANT TO FIND THE SOUTHWEST BOUNDARY OF THE LOUISIANA PURCHASE, AMONG OTHER THINGS...

MYSTERY SURROUNDS PIKE'S EXPEDITION TO COLORADO. AFTER THE TRANSFER OF LOUISIANA, GEN. WILKINSON BECAME GOVERNOR OF ALL THE PROVINCE — EXCEPT THE ORLEANS TERRITORY, THE PRESENT STATE OF LOUISIANA.

WILKINSON, TO SAY THE LEAST, IS A CONTROVERSIAL FIGURE IN LOUISIANA FRONTIER HISTORY. HISTORIANS SIMPLY CANNOT FIGURE OUT THE GENERAL...

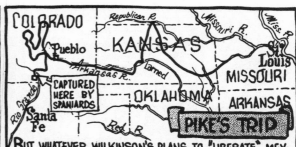

BUT WHATEVER WILKINSON'S PLANS TO "LIBERATE" MEXICO WITH OR WITHOUT AARON BURR, WHAT LIEUT. PIKE DID UNDER HIS COMMAND CONTRIBUTED A LOT TOWARD ESTABLISHING THE WESTERN LIMITS OF THE PURCHASE.

PIKE'S JOURNEY TO COLORADO WAS HIS SECOND IMPORTANT EXPEDITION. ONE YEAR EARLIER HE TRIED TO FIND THE SOURCE OF THE MISSISSIPPI IN MINNESOTA *IN MIDWINTER.*

HIS EXPLORATION OF COLORADO ALSO TOOK PLACE IN MID WINTER, AND AGAIN PIKE AND HIS MEN WERE WEARING SUMMER CLOTHES!

Stockade on Rio Grande, after description by Pike

BESIDES THE WEATHER, SOME HISTORIANS ARE ALSO COOL TOWARD PIKE AND HIS REAL OBJECTIVES. ALTHOUGH SEEKING THE SOURCE OF THE RED RIVER (BOUNDARY OF LOUISIANA), HE FOUND THE **RIO GRANDE**.

ON THANKSGIVING DAY, IN THE YEAR 1806, PIKE WAS TRYING TO CLIMB THE PEAK THAT NOW BEARS HIS NAME.

UNABLE TO SCALE THE PEAK, PIKE REPORTED IT WAS AN IMPOSSIBILITY. NOW TRAINS RUN UP THE FAMOUS PEAK ON REGULAR SCHEDULE. FARE: $5.75 UP & DOWN.

AT THE TIME OF THE PURCHASE, THE U.S. ARMY WAS CALLED *The* **LEGION** LEGIONNAIRES DRESSED FANCY IN BLUE FOR PARADES, BUT WORK CLOTHES ON THE WILD FRONTIER WAS THE HUNTING SHIRT. SUCH WAS THE SHIRT-SLEEVED GARB OF PIKE AND HIS MEN...

IN THEIR SUMMER CLOTHES, PIKE AND HIS MEN SPENT THE WINTER OF 1806-07 WANDERING THROUGH THE MOUNTAINS OF COLORADO. THESE U.S. SOLDIERS WERE PAID $5 A MONTH, REGULAR ARMY PAY.

IN JANUARY, 1807 THEY REACHED A RIVER WHICH PIKE DECIDED WAS THE RED — THE BOUNDARY BETWEEN LOUISIANA AND SPANISH SOIL. A STOCKADE WAS BUILT. "BUT WHY ON THE *SPANISH* SIDE?" ASK PUZZLED HISTORIANS.

THE RIVER WAS THE *RIO GRANDE!* THIS SECOND STOCKADE WAS FANCIER THAN THE FIRST IN PUEBLO, LACKING ONLY TWO CONVENIENCES — A DOOR AND A ROOF!

SITE OF PIKE'S RIO GRANDE STOCKADE, SECOND BUILDING IN COLORADO, IS NOW STATE-OWNED.

PIKE AND HIS MEN WERE "CAPTURED" BY THE SPANIARDS, WHO SHOWED THEM EVERY KINDNESS, GAVE DANCES FOR THEM NIGHTLY, AND LOANED PIKE $1000. THIS, ALSO, PUZZLES HISTORIANS...

EVERY ONE OF LIEUT. PIKE'S 15 TROOPS SURVIVED THE ZERO WINTER WEATHER OF COLORADO, THE DAYS WITHOUT ANY FOOD, AND THEN — IN MEXICO — THE SPANISH FIESTAS *EVERY* NIGHT. AT THE TIME OF THE LOUISIANA PURCHASE, U.S. SOLDIERS WERE *TOUGH*.

ALL THAT WAS MINE!

NAPOLEON'S LOUISIANA

BUT NAPOLEON HAD POSSESSION OF LOUISIANA FOR ONLY 20 DAYS ...AND IT TOOK 80 DAYS TO TELL HIM ABOUT IT.

THIS MAKES ME BOSS.

ON NOV. 29, 1803 LAUSSAT, NAPOLEON'S COLONIAL PREFECT IN NEW ORLEANS, RECEIVED THE KEYS TO FORTS ST. CHARLES AND ST. LOUIS.

THESE WOODEN FORTS STOOD ON THE RIVER ON EACH END OF NEW ORLEANS, AND NEITHER ONE HAD *EVER* FIRED A SHOT IN ANGER...

...BUT WHAT'S MORE IMPORTANT, NOBODY HAS EVER SHOT AT US.

I HAVE THE KEY TO THE FORT. SHOW ME THE LOCK.

LOCK? I DIDN'T KNOW IT HAD A DOOR.

AS ABSURD AS THESE FORTIFICATIONS AT NEW ORLEANS WAS THE 20-DAY FRENCH RULE OF LOUISIANA BY PETER LAUSSAT.

FORTIFICATIONS AROUND NEW ORLEANS IN 1803 HAD BEEN BUILT BY THE SPANIARDS AT THE TIME OF THE FRENCH REVOLUTION... TO KEEP FRENCHMEN IN, AND OHIO RIVER BOATMEN OUT.

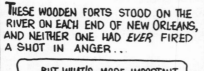

FT. BORGUNDY

New Orleans after 1791

FT. ST. JOHN

FT. ST. LOUIS

FT. ST. CHARLES

Mississippi R.

ON PAPER THEY LOOKED FORMIDABLE.

WARNING DON'T LEAN AGAINST THE FORT.

HOWEVER, THESE FORTIFICATIONS WERE NEVER MUCH MORE FORMIDABLE THAN PAPER.

GET SOME OF THE PALISADES, MEN — FOR KINDLING.

ONE YEAR AFTER THE PURCHASE, WILKINSON COMPLAINED TO THE U.S. SECRETARY OF WAR THAT ONE OF THE REAR FORTS WAS ACTUALLY STOLEN ONE DARK NIGHT —— FOR FIREWOOD.

THERE'LL BE SOME CHANGES MADE — BEFORE *I'M* CHANGED.

LAUSSAT BEGAN HIS 20-DAY ADMINISTRATION AS THOUGH IT WAS TO BE FOR 20 YEARS.

ILLUS. CABILDO

LAUSSAT

HE KICKED OUT THE SPANISH STYLE OF GOVERNMENT, AND SET UP A FRENCH SYSTEM.

ALSO, HE FIRED ALL THE SPANISH JUDGES, AND SOMEHOW HE FORGOT TO REPLACE *THEM.* WHEN THE U.S. TOOK OVER THERE WAS NO JUDICIARY AT ALL!

SPAIN MIGHT CAUSE TROUBLE, JEFFERSON THINKS.

WILKINSON

CLAIBORNE

YES, OUR'S MUST BE A *MILITARY* EXPEDITION.

NAPOLEON NEVER INTENDED FOR LAUSSAT TO RULE LOUISIANA FOR 20 DAYS. HE WAS SUPPOSED TO RECEIVE THE PROVINCE FROM SPAIN, AND TURN IT OVER TO THE U.S. ON THE SAME DAY. BUT IT TOOK 20 DAY LONGER FOR THE U.S. TO ORGANIZE ITS EXPEDITION TO RECEIVE – AND HOLD – LOUISIANA.

TELL 'EM TO FLY CLOSER I'M THE GOVERNOR.

AS GOVERNOR, LAUSSAT'S AUTHORITY WAS OVER *ALL* THE 900,000 SQUARE MILES OF LOUISIANA. BUT HIS ONLY TRIPS OUTSIDE OF NEW ORLEANS IN 1803 WAS FOR DUCK HUNTING.

TODAY, EVEN THE DUCKS DIDN'T REQUIRE ME.

HE MISSED!

BUT.. IN 1803 THERE WASN'T MUCH OF LOUISIANA OUTSIDE OF NEW ORLEANS THAT REQUIRED GOVERNING . . .

AT THE TIME OF THE PURCHASE, NEW ORLEANS WAS A CITY OF 8,056. THIS WAS 16% OF *ALL* THE INHABITANTS OF THE 900,000 SQ. MILES OF LOUISIANA.

U.S. *BIG* CITIES..1800	
PHILADELPHIA	69,403
NEW YORK	60,489
BOSTON	24,937
CHARLESTON	20,473
PITTSBURGH	1,565
CINCINNATI	750
LOUISVILLE	359

U.S. POPULATION JUST BEFORE THE PURCHASE WAS 5,305,925.

ALREADY WE GOT 45,000 PEOPLE IN OHIO.. AND 4,763 IN MICHIGAN TERRITORY!

WHEW! THAT'S GROWTH FOR YOU!

IF SPAIN STARTS ANY TROUBLE, IT'LL BE AT NATCHITOCHES.

IT'S THE FRONTIER.

SETTLEMENTS IN LOUISIANA OUTSIDE OF NEW ORLEANS AND ST. LOUIS WERE CALLED "POSTS". AFTER THE PURCHASE THE MOST IMPORTANT POST WAS NATCHITOCHES, THE *FIRST* SETTLEMENT IN ALL LOUISIANA.

WE'VE GOT TO HAVE TRADE..

IN 1713, WHEN CADILLAC WHO FOUNDED DETROIT WAS GOVERNOR OF LOUISIANA, HE SENT A CANADIAN COUREUR DE BOIS NAMED ST. DENIS OFF TO ESTABLISH NATCHITOCHES ON THE RED RIVER.

First Permanent Settlement, Louisiana Purchase

FRENCH LOUISIANA WAS EAGER TO TRADE WITH SPANISH MEXICO. NATCHITOCHES WAS AN ADVANCE TRADING POST.

WELL . . . TRAFFIC SHOULD BE LIGHT.

BETWEEN THIS FRENCH POST AND THE NEAREST SPANISH SETTLEMENT ON THE RIO GRANDE WAS 500 MILES OF GREAT OPEN SPACE! THIS WAS TEXAS IN 1714, AND ITS OWNERSHIP WAS IN DISPUTE.

HOW COME NO RECORDS?

I COULDN'T SPELL NATCHITOCHES.

HISTORIAN

HISTORIANS KNOW LITTLE OF EXPLORER LOUIS J. de ST. DENIS WHO WALKED BACK AND FORTH ACROSS THE STATE OF TEXAS OVER 200 YEARS AGO.

ST. DENIS IS THE NAME – I HAPPENED TO BE IN TEXAS..

AND LITTLE WAS KNOWN OF TEXAS THAT DAY IN AUGUST, 1714 WHEN ST. DENIS APPEARED AT THE SPANISH POST ON THE RIO GRANDE.

NEXT TUESDAY.

PLEASED TO MEET YOU, SENORITA... WHEN WILL YOU MARRY ME?

ST. DENIS ALMOST IMMEDIATELY DEMONSTRATED GOOD INTENTIONS BY MARRYING THE GRAND DAUGHTER OF THE COMMANDING OFFICER.

I WAS THE *FIRST* BOOSTER OF TEXAS...

ALSO, ST. DENIS URGED THE SPANIARDS TO SETTLE IN TEXAS, AND OFFERED TO HELP 'EM MOVE.

St. Denis actually did direct Spanish establishment of **NACOGDOCHES** in Texas in 1716.

Nacogdoches in East Texas is near Natchitoches in Louisiana. St. Denis planned it this way for trading convenience. But the Spaniards thought it was to guard Texas from Frenchmen.

After reporting to Gov. Cadillac in Mobile, St. Denis loaded mules with goods and hurried back to the Rio Grande.

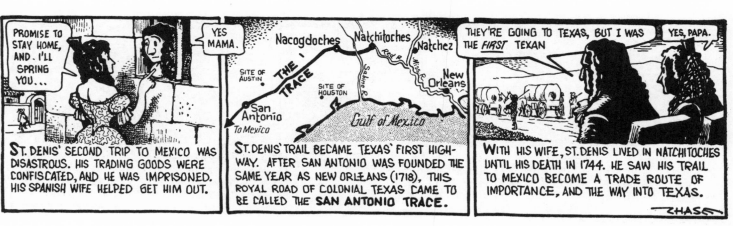

St. Denis' second trip to Mexico was disastrous. His trading goods were confiscated, and he was imprisoned. His Spanish wife helped get him out.

St. Denis' trail became Texas' first highway. After San Antonio was founded the same year as New Orleans (1718), this royal road of colonial Texas came to be called the **SAN ANTONIO TRACE**.

With his wife, St. Denis lived in Natchitoches until his death in 1744. He saw his trail to Mexico become a trade route of importance, and the way into Texas.

Via St. Denis' San Antonio Trace, Lieut. Pike's expedition returned to Louisiana in 1807. Later, it became the route of Anglo-American settlers into Texas.

But before Pike's return, the U.S. had established a strong garrison at Natchitoches. Spaniards were not allowed across the Sabine River.

BUT... for forty years after the purchase the western boundary of Louisiana was unsettled. Spanish claims were inherited by (1) the Mexican Republic, and (2) the Texas Republic.

Largely because of the exploits of St. Denis in Texas, France maintained that the western boundary of Louisiana was the Rio Grande, and Rockies.

Laussat, who ruled Louisiana for 20 days in 1803, declared his domain extended to the Rio Grande. Later, Jefferson became convinced Texas was included in the Louisiana Purchase...

But things happened... had it not been for the War of 1812, the U.S. would have surely latched on to Texas as purchased land. Then, in 1819, when Florida was ceded to the U.S., all American claims to Texas were surrendered.

IN DECEMBER 1803, GOV. CLAIBORNE AND GEN. WILKINSON WERE APPROACHING NEW ORLEANS WITH ABOUT 500 PICKED-MEN TO RECEIVE THE LOUISIANA PURCHASE FOR THE UNITED STATES.

THE PAY IS $5 A MONTH, AND KEEP. ALSO, YOU GET FREE TRANSPORTATION ON A BARGE.

JOIN THE ARMY AND SEE NEW ORLEANS

GEE! THIS MUST BE MY LUCKY DAY!

THESE PICKED MEN HAD BEEN PICKED UP ANYWHERE CLAIBORNE AND WILKINSON COULD ENLIST THEM ON THE MISSISSIPPI AND TENNESSEE FRONTIER. CLAIBORNE HAS REPORTED THEY WERE ILL-CLAD, BUT THEY COULD SHOOT STRAIGHT WITH THEIR LONG RIFLES...

ADVANCE BASE FOR THE EXPEDITION THAT MARCHED ON NEW ORLEANS IN 1803 WAS FORT ADAMS, 50 MILES SOUTH OF NATCHEZ ON THE MISSISSIPPI RIVER.

FORT ADAMS, ON THE WEST FLORIDA BORDER GUARDED THE SOUTHWEST FRONTIER OF THE UNITED STATES BEFORE THE PURCHASE OF LOUISIANA.

REMEMBER, YOU GUYS! WE'RE GOING TO NEW ORLEANS TO MAKE HISTORY - NOT WHOOPEE.

AW HECK, SARGE!

AMERICAN OFFICIALS WORRIED THAT SPAIN MIGHT BLOCK THE TRANSFER OF LOUISIANA. THE U.S. EXPEDITIONARY FORCE TO NEW ORLEANS IN DEC. 1803 WAS ALERTED TO BE ON GUARD FOR ANY EVENTUALITY.

THIS DOESN'T EXACTLY MAKE US WAR-MONGERS.

FOR TAKING POSSESSION OF LOUISIANA, AGAINST ALL ODDS...

$10,000

TO RAISE THE ARMY, EQUIP IT, AND TO PAY ALL COSTS OF A MILITARY OCCUPATION OF NEW ORLEANS IN DECEMBER, 1803, CONGRESS HAD APPROPRIATED $10,000.

YONDER'S NEW ORLEANS, MEN — AROUND THE NEXT BEND OF THE RIVER!

ON DEC. 16, 1803 WILKINSON WITH 300 REGULARS PITCHED CAMP ON THE OUTSKIRTS OF NEW ORLEANS. CLAIBORNE WOULD ARRIVE THE NEXT DAY.

HOW COME YOU'RE A CAVALRY MAN, MAC?

ON ACCOUNT OF ME, THAT'S HOW COME.

MAC'S

CLAIBORNE BROUGHT THE REST OF THE EXPEDITIONARY FORCE. SOME OF THE TROOPS WERE CAVALRYMEN. THIS WAS BECAUSE THEY HAD ENLISTED WITH THEIR HORSES.

GOV. CLAIBORNE'S COMPLIMENTS, SIR.

ON DECEMBER 17, 1803, THE AMERICAN ARMY OF OCCUPATION WAS ENCAMPED ON THE OUTSKIRTS OF NEW ORLEANS. LAUSSAT, THE FRENCH PREFECT, WAS DULY INFORMED.

GOV. CLAIBORNE AND GEN. WILKINSON, WITH THIRTY HORSEMEN RODE INTO NEW ORLEANS TO FORMALLY GREET LAUSSAT. THEN LAUSSAT RODE OUT TO REPAY THE FORMAL CALL.

OH.. IT'S MR. LAUSSAT.

OUI, MONSIEUR SENTRY.

WHAT TIME IS DINNER?

IN SPITE OF ALL THE HORSE BACK RIDING, A DATE FOR THE TRANSFER OF LOUISIANA WAS SET — DECEMBER 20...

SPAIN COULD HAVE STARTED A WAR IN NEW ORLEANS AT THIS TIME. SPANISH OFFICIALS AND *TROOPS* WERE STILL THERE. BUT THE OUTNUMBERED AMERICANS WERE NOT ATTACKED.

WE'RE NOT A-GOING TO MAKE A MARDI GRAS PARADE OUT OF THIS, SARGE?

THE CITIZEN SOLDIERS OF THE U.S. FRONTIER TOOK A DIM VIEW OF PARTICIPATING IN ANY *FORMAL CEREMONY* FOR THE TRANSFER OF THE LOUISIANA PURCHASE.

THIS PURCHASE MAKES THE U.S. A GREAT NATION. YOU U.S. SOLDIERS *MUST HAVE* SPIT AND POLISH.

HECK, I GOT SPIT. ME, TOO.

DEC. 20, 1803 ORDER OF THE DAY

NEVERTHELESS, ORDERS WERE ISSUED. TO THE BEAT OF DRUMS, U.S. TROOPS WOULD MARCH INTO THE CITY AND PARADE TO THE *PLACE D'ARMES* ...

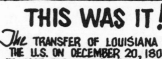

THIS WAS IT!

THE TRANSFER OF LOUISIANA TO THE U.S. ON DECEMBER 20, 1803. AT LEAST, THIS IS THE WAY THE SWEDISH ARTIST, THURE DE THULSTRUP, IMAGINED HOW IT LOOKED — 100 YEARS LATER.

THE ORIGINAL OF THIS WIDELY REPRODUCED PAINTING HANGS IN THE CABILDO IN NEW ORLEANS — THE BUILDING ON THE LEFT ...

HEY MAC, DID YOU SEE OUR 'PIT'CHER'?

WE SURE WUZ PRETTY.

HOW COME I DIDN'T LOOK LIKE I DID IN THE PAINTING, SARGE?

QUIT GRIPPING. YOU DID - 100 YEARS LATER.

MR. THULSTRUP WAS AN ABLE HISTORICAL ILLUSTRATOR. HIS U.S. ARMY UNIFORMS OF 1803 ARE CORRECT IN EVERY DETAIL. SOLDIERS WHO CAME WITH CLAIBORNE AND WILKINSON *SHOULD* HAVE LOOKED AS MR. THULSTRUP HAS PAINTED THEM.

IN A SENSE, THE U.S. OCCUPATION OF NEW ORLEANS IN DEC. 1803, WAS A NAVAL OPERATION THE AMERICANS CAME IN FLATBOATS

THERE IS ON THE GLOBE ONE SPOT, THE POSSESSOR OF WHICH IS OUR NATURAL AND HABITUAL ENEMY. IT IS NEW ORLEANS ...

TO JEFFERSON, NEW ORLEANS WAS THE REASON FOR THE PURCHASE — AND THE MISSISSIPPI VALLEY WAS THE REASON FOR NEW ORLEANS.

NEW ORLEANS, ALWAYS, HAS REFLECTED THE GREATNESS OF THE MISSISSIPPI VALLEY. THIS IS THE HISTORIC ROLE OF PORT CITIES. BUT IN DEC. 1803, HISTORY STOOD STILL FOR A WHILE, DOWN IN NEW ORLEANS.

DON'T START ANY TROUBLE, MEN. WE'RE IN A TIGHT SPOT

THE NAVAL OPERATION THAT LANDED ABOUT 500 AMERICANS AT NEW ORLEANS IN DEC. 1803, ONLY ESTABLISHED A *BEACHHEAD!*

WE'RE JUST WATCHING

THE MONTHS FOLLOWING THE TRANSFER OF LOUISIANA WERE TRYING ONES FOR GOV. CLAIBORNE. *BOTH* THE SPANISH AND THE FRENCH GOVERNORS REMAINED IN TOWN. NOBODY KNEW WHY?

AMERICANS SLEEP HERE, SENORS.

ALSO, SPANISH TROOPS, OUTNUMBERING GEN. WILKINSON'S U.S. FORCE, HAD THE BEST ACCOMMODATIONS IN THE BARRACKS. AMERICAN TROOPS WERE ALLOWED IN THE BARRACK BASEMENT *ONLY*.

THE HECTIC TOUCH-AND-GO DAYS FOLLOWING THE TRANSFER WERE ECONOMICALLY AS WELL AS POLITICALLY CONFUSING. THERE WAS NO MONEY!

HOW MUCH FOR EGGS, MR. RENE?

HOW MUCH OF *WHAT*?

SPAIN HAD ALL THE DOLLARS IN 1803. AS A SPANISH CITY, NEW ORLEANS HAD JINGLED FINANCIALLY WITH SILVER PIECES-OF-EIGHT. AFTER 20 DAYS OF FRENCH RULE, AND NOW AMERICAN ...EVERYBODY WONDERED *WHAT* WAS MONEY?

HISTORIANS ARE SNOOPY PEOPLE!

WHEN LAUSSAT TOOK OVER FOR FRANCE, HE ALSO TOOK OVER $15,636.50 IN SPANISH COIN. HISTORIANS HAVE BEEN LOOKING FOR THIS SUM OF MONEY EVER SINCE...

CHASE

x! IF I HADN'T PROMISED THE SARGE.

SPANISH TROOPS, IN GREATER NUMBER THAN THE AMERICANS, STAYED ON IN NEW ORLEANS FOR FOUR MONTHS AFTER THE TRANSFER TO THE U.S.A.

THAT'S IT, HONEY!

BUT IT WAS NOT FROM THE SPANIARDS THAT THE FIRST TROUBLE CAME.. IT WAS THE CREOLES, THOSE FRENCH AND SPANISH NATIVES. THEY OBJECTED TO HAVING SQUARE DANCES!

WE WALTZ, M'SIEUR.

I G-GUESS YOU FELLOWS WANNA CUT IN, EH?

THERE WAS A NEAR-RIOT OVER THE SQUARE DANCING. THE CREOLES INSISTED IT WAS AN ENGLISH DANCE; THEREFORE, ANTI-FRENCH.

CHASE

UNCLE SAM GOT AN EMPTY STOCKING ON HIS FIRST CHRISTMAS IN LOUISIANA

THE SPANISH TREASURY WAS EMPTY!

CHASE

MY, MY – THESE BILLS ADD UP TO EXACTLY $15,636.50!

LAUSSAT MUST HAVE INCURRED SOME HEAVY EXPENSES DURING HIS 20-DAY ADMINISTRATION. ACCORDING TO COUNCIL RECORDS, THERE WAS NOT A NICKEL OF THE $15,636.50 OF SPANISH MONIES TO TRANSFER TO THE AMERICANS...

I'LL OPEN IT BUT YOU'LL BE SORRY...

NO. 3

THIS $15,636.50 HAD COME FROM TWO SPANISH CHESTS. EACH OF THE FUNDS HAD A SPECIAL KEEPER. THERE WAS ALSO A *THIRD* CHEST, BUT IT WAS A SURPRISE PACKAGE!

HUM'PH!

UNCLE SAM GOT A LOT WHEN HE GOT THE LOUISIANA TERRITORY – BUT HE *DIDN'T* GET ANY OF THE SILVER SPANISH DOLLARS IN 1803

CHASE

RENT

CHURCH

MONIES LAUSSAT TOOK OVER WHEN HE TOOK OVER LOUISIANA, CAME FROM RENTS PAID THE GOVERNMENT ($12,600), AND THE CHURCH BOX ($3,036.50)

A THIRD CHEST WAS CALLED "DEPOSITS"

KEEPER OF THE THIRD CHEST ANNOUNCED IT SHOULD CONTAIN $9,000; IF IT WASN'T EMPTY. EVEN THE SPANISH GOVERNOR HAD BORROWED FROM IT, LEAVING – AS SECURITY – $2000 IN COUNTERFEIT PAPER MONEY. THE GOVERNOR BORROWED $1,570 IN SILVER.

DEPOSITS, IT SAYS

IOU IOU IOU

NO.3

HECK, SOME DIDN'T EVEN LEAVE ME PHONY SECURITIES!

NEXT
HOW IOWA GOT TO BE IOWA

DEC. 28, 1846 IS THE BIRTHDAY OF THE STATE OF ...AYU-HBA

THAT'S WHAT I CALLED IT

MAYBE WE DON'T SPELL 'EM GOOD...

BUT WE DO SPELL 'EM SIMPLE!

LIKE ALL INDIAN NAMES, IOWA HAS HAD MANY SPELLINGS. LASALLE WROTE IT AIOUNONEA. LEWIS AND CLARK WROTE IAWAY. LIEUTENANT PIKE WAS FIRST TO WRITE THE NAME IOWA.

IT'S 4 A.M. AND I'M ALREADY AT MY CHORES.

4 A.M. -UGH!

THIS SIOUX INDIAN WORD MEANS "THE SLEEPY ONES." BUT IOWA'S DEFINITION IS NO LONGER ANY MORE RECOGNIZABLE THAN ITS FIRST SPELLING.

ZHASE

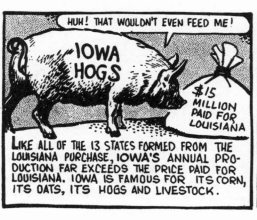

HUH! THAT WOULDN'T EVEN FEED ME!

IOWA HOGS

$15 MILLION PAID FOR LOUISIANA

LIKE ALL OF THE 13 STATES FORMED FROM THE LOUISIANA PURCHASE, IOWA'S ANNUAL PRODUCTION FAR EXCEEDS THE PRICE PAID FOR LOUISIANA. IOWA IS FAMOUS FOR ITS CORN, ITS OATS, ITS HOGS AND LIVESTOCK.

JUST WHAT I WANTED—I ONLY HAVE 28 STATES.

ADMITTED TO THE UNION DURING THE CHRISTMAS HOLIDAYS IN 1846, IOWA CAME AS A CHRISTMAS PRESENT TO UNCLE SAM.

ZHASE

GEE..

..IF I JUST HAD SOMEBODY TO SEW 'EM ON.

IOWA BUTTONS

IOWA IS WELL QUALIFIED TO BUTTON UP THIS STORY OF THE LOUISIANA PURCHASE. FOR IOWA HAS A BUTTON INDUSTRY! AT ONE TIME IOWA PROVIDED 20% OF ALL UNCLE SAM'S BUTTONS!

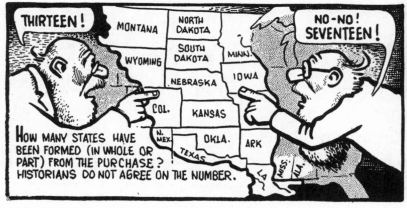

THIRTEEN!

NO-NO! SEVENTEEN!

HOW MANY STATES HAVE BEEN FORMED (IN WHOLE OR PART) FROM THE PURCHASE? HISTORIANS DO NOT AGREE ON THE NUMBER.

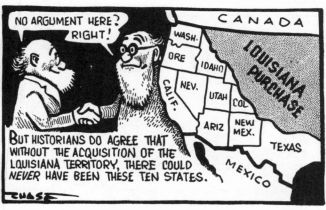

NO ARGUMENT HERE? RIGHT!

BUT HISTORIANS DO AGREE THAT WITHOUT THE ACQUISITION OF THE LOUISIANA TERRITORY, THERE COULD NEVER HAVE BEEN THESE TEN STATES.

ZHASE

IN THE BEGINNING, ALL THE MISSISSIPPI VALLEY WAS LOUISIANA. AFTER THE REVOLUTION THE UNITED STATES GOT HALF OF IT FREE. THEN, THE WESTERN HALF WAS PURCHASED

HALF WAS A BARGAIN.

WESTERN LOUISIANA PURCHASED IN 1803

EASTERN LOUISIANA FREE! (IN 1783)

...AND HALF WAS A "STEAL"

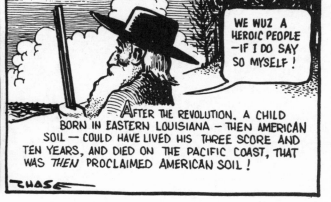

WE WUZ A HEROIC PEOPLE—IF I DO SAY SO MYSELF!

AFTER THE REVOLUTION, A CHILD BORN IN EASTERN LOUISIANA—THEN AMERICAN SOIL—COULD HAVE LIVED HIS THREE SCORE AND TEN YEARS, AND DIED ON THE PACIFIC COAST, THAT WAS THEN PROCLAIMED AMERICAN SOIL!

ZHASE

OUT HERE, HONEY – WE'RE JUST CITIZENS OF THE U-NITED STATES OF AMERICA..

U.S. PUBLIC LANDS

THE PENNSYLVANIANS, THE VIRGINIANS, THE NEW ENGLANDERS, THE NEW YORKERS AND CAROLINIANS, *ALL* WHO FIRST SETTLED IN THE OHIO VALLEY WERE, INDEED, A HEROIC PEOPLE. IN THE WILDERNESS OF EASTERN LOUISIANA THEY BECAME **ONE** PEOPLE!

—CHASE

WE CALL 'EM AMERICANS..

SETTLERS WHO VENTURED DOWN THE RIVER TO NEW ORLEANS, PORT OF THE VALLEY, WERE CALLED BY SPANISH AND FRENCH COLONISTS THERE – *THE AMERICANS.*

PEOPLE CAN WORK WONDERS WHEN THEY'RE *FREE* PEOPLE.

WE PROVED IT!

ALONE IN THE WILDERNESS THESE PEOPLE THEY CALLED AMERICANS LEARNED TO DEPEND UPON THEMSELVES. THEIR ENERGY, ENTERPRISE, AND AMAZING INGENUITY BECAME CHARACTERISTICS FOREVER AFTERWARDS TERMED "AMERICAN."

THE SAME BREED OF AMERICANS WHO WON THE WILDERNESS PUSHED ON INTO THE WESTERN PLAINS, OVER THE ROCKIES, TO THE PACIFIC... AND THEY ALTERED THEIR IMPLEMENTS TO THE NEW COUNTRY — CONESTOGA WAGONS BECAME PRAIRIE SCHOONERS...

I COULD SHOOT AND LOAD THIS ON HOSSBACK..

ALSO, THE FRONTIERSMAN CHANGED HIS WEAPON...

THIS IS THE COLT 44 SIX-SHOOTER, FIRST USED BY THE TEXAS RANGERS. THIS MODEL WAS 15½ INCHES LONG.

GEE!

BUT IF THERE HADN'T BEEN A LOUISIANA PURCHASE IN 1803 THERE MAY *NEVER* HAVE BEEN A WILD WEST, WITH SIX-SHOOTERS, AND STUFF! THINK THAT OVER, KIDS.

HERE ENDS THIS LOUISIANA PURCHASE STORY. SO LONG, EVERYBODY! JOHN CHASE.

HELLO *AGAIN* EVERYBODY...

1953 Louisiana Purchase Story By John Chase

THIS 1953 STORY ENDED WITH THE STRIP ABOVE. BUT A 1982 STORY CANNOT, AS THE THREE BELOW HASTEN TO REMIND US.

I'M A FORGOTTEN FOUNDING FATHER – FINALLY REMEMBERED.

FIRST AS A COMIC STRIP SYNDICATED FROM COAST TO COAST IN 1953, FOLLOWED BY SIX EDITIONS OF THE STRIPS IN BOOK FORM, LIKE THE LOUISIANA PURCHASE ITSELF – ITS STORY GOES ON AND **ON.**

LOUISIANA PURCHASE

THESE BOARDS, UPON WHICH THIS STORY WAS TOLD IN 1953, WERE DONATED TO TULANE UNIVERSITY LIBRARY. ALL WERE BORROWED BACK FOR EDITING, UPDATING, ETC.

IN 1908, THE DISCOVERY BY A REMARKABLE BLACK COWBOY, NEAR FOLSOM IN NEW MEXICO, WAS TO PROVE THE AMERICAN INDIANS 10,000 YEARS **OLDER.**

THERE'S MUCH **MORE** TO SAY ABOUT ME TOO.

OL' MAN RIVER

—THEN THE STRIPS THAT FOLLOW HAVE BEEN ADDED TO THE STORY. **READ ON...**

AMERICA HAD MANY **FOUNDING FATHERS** — MOST ALL OF THEM ARE REMEMBERED.

BUT *EVERYBODY* FORGOT **OLIVER POLLOCK** — AN IMPORTANT LEADER IN THE AMERICAN REVOLUTION — THIS IS POLLOCK'S ONLY LIKENESS, DRAWN FROM DESCRIPTIONS HIS DESCENDANTS PROVIDED.

BAM!

ON 1862, DURING THE CIVIL WAR, THE U.S. NAVY DESTROYED POLLOCK'S ONLY PORTRAIT, WHEN IT DESTROYED THE TOWN OF BAYOU SARA ON THE RIVER.

I WAS THERE

THE THREE AMERICAN REVOLUTIONS

Mississippi River — "POLLOCK'S PURCHASE" — CLARK — LOUISIANA — THIRTEEN COLONIES — THE WAR WASHINGTON WON — FLORIDA WAR GALVEZ WON

OLIVER POLLOCK PLAYED A MAJOR ROLE IN ALL THREE.

AS FOURTH LARGEST CONTRIBUTOR TO THE AMERICAN CAUSE, POLLOCK WORKED WITH ROBT. MORRIS TO KEEP WASHINGTON SUPPLIED. ALONE HE FINANCED CLARK'S WAR IN ILLINOIS. AND IN 1779 HE MARCHED WITH GALVEZ (LEFT) IN HIS WAR IN FLORIDA.

Baton Rouge Sept. 21, 1779 Dear Folks: Surrender Natchez by return mail. O. Pollock

O.K. OLIVER.

ALSO, FROM BATON ROUGE, INFLUENTIAL POLLOCK CAPTURED NATCHEZ BY MAIL.

HE WAS MY DOLLAR-A-YEAR-MAN BEFORE I HAD A DOLLAR.

UNCLE SAM

I'M OLIVER POLLOCK... I MADE THE FIRST DOLLAR SIGN — I THINK.

BEGINNING LONG BEFORE THE PURCHASE, THE SPANISH "PESO," WHICH MEANS "PIECE", WAS THE ONLY MONEY IN LOUISIANA — AND THERE WAS A "PESO SIGN." (AN 'S' WRITTEN OVER A 'P'.)

IT'S EASY TO SEE HOW THE DOLLAR SIGN BEGAN WITH THE PESO SIGN. AND BEST SOURCES INDICATE POLLOCK PIONEERED ITS POPULARITY.

IT DOESN'T STEM FROM 8 INTO $ — AND IT'S NOT U.S. LIKE THIS $ — BUT AS FOR THE PESO... HM-M?

THE "BEST SOURCES" MENTIONED ABOVE IS ONE MAN — PROFESSOR FLORIAN CAJORI. IN 1912, REPORT OF HIS YEARS-LONG RESEARCH RAN IN *THE SCIENTIFIC MONTHLY*.

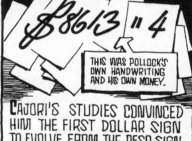

$8613 " 4

THIS WAS POLLOCK'S OWN HANDWRITING AND HIS OWN MONEY.

CAJORI'S STUDIES CONVINCED HIM THE FIRST DOLLAR SIGN TO EVOLVE FROM THE PESO SIGN WAS IN A POLLOCK LETTER TO GENERAL CLARK SEPT, 12, 1778.

SURE, I THINK OLIVER WAS FIRST.

IT'S UNLIKELY PROF. CAJORI EVER HEARD OF THE PERE CYRILLO, POLLOCK'S FRIEND AND PASTOR. IN 1779, HE CARVED THIS DOLLAR SIGN FOR HIS FRIEND. IT SURE BACKS UP CAJORI'S RESEARCH...

THE PERE'S DOLLAR SIGN CARVING IS NOW IN THE MUSEUM OF THE N.O. URSULINE CONVENT.

PESO $. Dollar Sign

SYMBOL FOR THE NEW DOLLAR — OLIVER POLLOCK NEW ORLEANS 1779

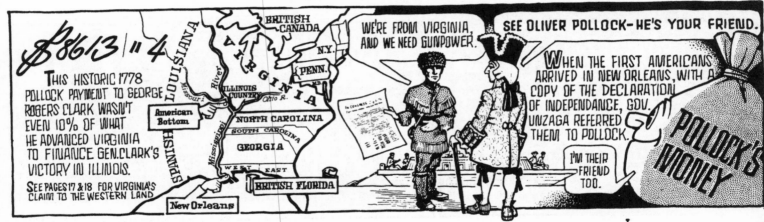

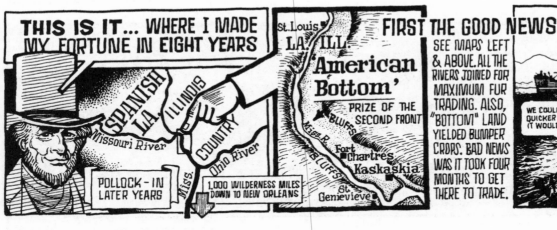

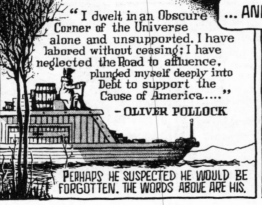

IT'S TAKEN 180 YEARS FOR ANOTHER NOTED VISITOR TO REACH THE AMERICAN BOTTOM

American People THAT WAS ME!

US INDIANS WERE THERE FIRST.

BY 1980 THE CENTER OF POPULATION WAS IN MISSOURI.

PICTURE THE USA AS A WEIGHTLESS BOARD, WITH ALL THE PEOPLE ON IT WHERE THEY LIVE. BALANCE THE BOARD ON A PIN, AND THAT IS THE CENTER OF POPULATION. (AT TIME OF THE PURCHASE, IT WAS WASHINGTON, D.C.)

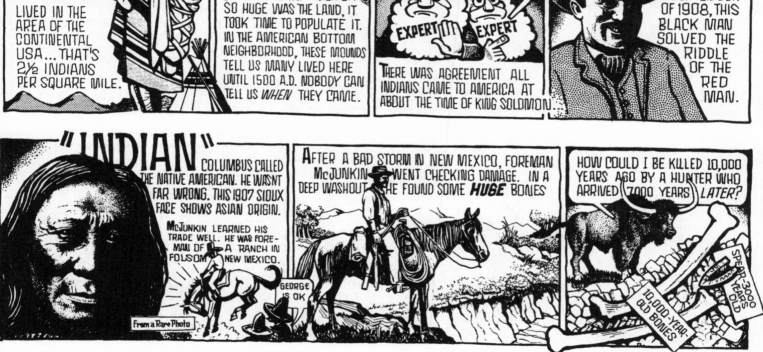

BEFORE COLUMBUS, 846,000 INDIANS LIVED IN THE AREA OF THE CONTINENTAL USA... THAT'S 2½ INDIANS PER SQUARE MILE.

PAPOOSE ONLY ONE HALF INDIAN...

Cahokia Mounds

IN PREHISTORIC AMERICA SO HUGE WAS THE LAND, IT TOOK TIME TO POPULATE IT. IN THE AMERICAN BOTTOM NEIGHBORHOOD, THESE MOUNDS TELL US MANY LIVED HERE UNTIL 1500 A.D. NOBODY CAN TELL US WHEN THEY CAME.

INDIANS HERE 3,000 YEARS. NO MORE THAN THAT!

EXPERT EXPERT

THERE WAS AGREEMENT ALL INDIANS CAME TO AMERICA AT ABOUT THE TIME OF KING SOLOMON.

I'M GEORGE McJUNKIN.

THEN, IN SEPTEMBER OF 1908, THIS BLACK MAN SOLVED THE RIDDLE OF THE RED MAN.

"INDIAN" COLUMBUS CALLED THE NATIVE AMERICAN. HE WASN'T FAR WRONG. THIS 1907 SIOUX FACE SHOWS ASIAN ORIGIN.

McJUNKIN LEARNED HIS TRADE WELL. HE WAS FOREMAN OF A RANCH IN FOLSOM, NEW MEXICO.

From a Rare Photo

GEORGE IS OK

AFTER A BAD STORM IN NEW MEXICO, FOREMAN McJUNKIN WENT CHECKING DAMAGE. IN A DEEP WASHOUT HE FOUND SOME HUGE BONES

HOW COULD I BE KILLED 10,000 YEARS AGO BY A HUNTER WHO ARRIVED 7,000 YEARS LATER?

SPEAR-3,000 YEARS OLD

10,000-YEAR-OLD BONES

NO LESS CONFUSED THAN THE BISON—EXTINCT 10,000 YEARS BEING KILLED 7,000 YEARS LATER—WERE THE EXPERTS. THEY HAD TO FINALLY REVISE THEIR FIGURES. McJUNKIN'S FIND WAS TOO CONVINCING!

OK-OK, INDIANS IN AMERICA OVER 10,000 YEARS!

EXPERTS

ASIA

LAND BRIDGE

THEY CAME DURING THE ICE AGE WHEN THE SEAS WERE 200 FEET LOWER.

THE FIRST "INDIAN TRAIL"

THIS WAS IT! THROUGH THE MELTING ICE PACK TO THE PRESENT-DAY AREA OF THE U.S.A.

ICE ICE

UNITED STATES

ENDED IN LOUISIANA

MAPS SHOW HOW "TRAIL" ENTERED U.S.A. IN LOUISIANA PURCHASE STATES. (SEE THE ARROW.)

PREHISTORIC SPEARS NAMED FOR N.M. TOWNS WHERE FOUND

WYOMING NEB. IOWA UTAH COL. KANSAS MO. ILL. OKLA. NEW MEXICO TEXAS MISS LA. MEXICO

FOLSOM CLOVIS

Don BERNARDO de GALVEZ

HE WAS THE MOST POPULAR OF LOUISIANA'S EIGHT SPANISH GOVERNORS. HE MARRIED A CREOLE, FÉLICIE DE LA MAXENT d'ESTREHAN, AND NAMED ALL WEST FLORIDA IN HER HONOR. THEN, FOR HIM, LOUISIANA HAS NAMED ONE OF ITS PARISHES "SAINT BERNARD."

FELICIANA

ST. BERNARD PARISH

IMPORTANT WAS HIS VICTORY OVER THE ENGLISH IN WEST FLORIDA...

NOTABLE, TOO, WAS HIS WORK IN SETTLING VACANT LANDS OUTSIDE NEW ORLEANS. BESIDES ST. BERNARD, HE DID MUCH FOR CAJUN PRAIRIE CATTLEMEN.

TO TEMPT MORE SETTLERS, GALVEZ NOT ONLY GAVE THEM LAND BUT ALSO AN AXE, SHOVEL, HOE, SICKLE, TWO HENS AND A ROOSTER, A COW, TWO PIGS AND FOOD...

BUT THE COW'S ONLY A LOAN

FOOD FOR A YEAR

PRICE $4

$13 AND UP

MEXICO

NEW ORLEANS

BUT...IN THE CAJUN PRAIRIE, CATTLE WAS THE BIG MONEY CROP. COWS BOUGHT FOR $4 WERE MARKETED FOR $13, AND MORE. BUT THE TRAIL HOME PASSED THROUGH THE RISKY ATTAKAPAS COUNTRY, WHERE THE INDIANS ATE COWS— AND COWBOYS TOO!

ATTAKAPAS COUNTRY WAS IN LOUISIANA. NAMES OF BAYOUS SHOWN WERE ALL NAMES OF ATTAKAPAS CHIEFS BY 1803 THESE CANNIBALS HAD ABOUT LOST THEIR TASTE FOR CAJUNS.

THAT'S US CHIEFS ALL OVER!

SABINE · CALCASIEU · LACASSINE · NEZPIQUE · MERMENTAU · QUEUE DE TORTUE · ATCHAFALAYA · TECHE

ME LIKE TO HAVE YOU FOR DINNER.

NO—ME WANT YOU FOR DINNER.

$61,148.68 FOR CAJUNS

GOV. MIRO—WHO CAME AFTER GALVEZ WAS EVEN NICER TO CAJUNS...

IN 1885, THE LAST TWO ATTAKAPAS WERE LIVING NEAR LAKE CHARLES. THEN THEY DISAPPEARED. ONE HISTORIAN SUSPECTS THAT—LIKE THE GINGHAM DOG AND CALLICO CAT—THEY SIMPLY ATE EACH OTHER UP.

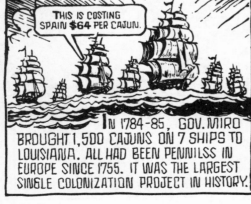

THIS IS COSTING SPAIN $64 PER CAJUN.

IN 1784-85, GOV. MIRO BROUGHT 1,500 CAJUNS ON 7 SHIPS TO LOUISIANA. ALL HAD BEEN PENNILSS IN EUROPE SINCE 1755. IT WAS THE LARGEST SINGLE COLONIZATION PROJECT IN HISTORY.

OUACHITA · RAPIDES · POINTE COUPEE · IBERVILLE · ATTAKAPAS · LAFOURCHE · LAKE · GERMAN COAST · N.O. · ORLEANS

IN 1805, WHEN LOUISIANA WAS FIRST CARVED INTO "COUNTIES"—ONE WAS NAMED ACADIA.

ALL SETTLED UPRIVER FROM NEW ORLEANS.

WE HOPE GOVERNOR MIRO DOESN'T SUE THE CAJUNS.

ALSO IN 1785, FORT MIRO WAS FOUNDED ON THE OUACHITA RIVER. BUT IN 1819, THE FIRST STEAMBOAT CAME UP THE RIVER, AND FORT MIRO'S NAME BE BECAME MONROE-NAME OF THE STEAMBOAT.

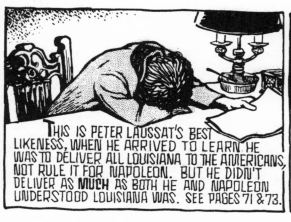

THIS IS PETER LAUSSAT'S BEST LIKENESS, WHEN HE ARRIVED TO LEARN HE WAS TO DELIVER ALL LOUISIANA TO THE AMERICANS, NOT RULE IT FOR NAPOLEON. BUT HE DIDN'T DELIVER AS **MUCH** AS BOTH HE AND NAPOLEON UNDERSTOOD LOUISIANA WAS. SEE PAGES 71 & 73.

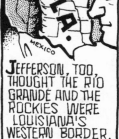

THAT WAS IT...

JEFFERSON, TOO, THOUGHT THE RIO GRANDE AND THE ROCKIES WERE LOUISIANA'S WESTERN BORDER.

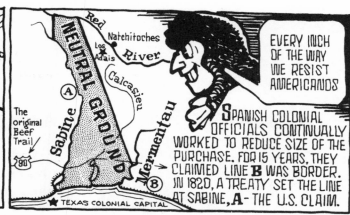

EVERY INCH OF THE WAY WE RESIST AMERICANDS

SPANISH COLONIAL OFFICIALS CONTINUALLY WORKED TO REDUCE SIZE OF THE PURCHASE. FOR 15 YEARS, THEY CLAIMED LINE **B** WAS BORDER. IN 1820, A TREATY SET THE LINE AT SABINE, **A** - THE U.S. CLAIM.

IT TOOK 432 YEARS TO PROVE, BUT I WAS RIGHT ABOUT **HIM**!

(SEE PAGE 81)

CARTOONISTS, WHO SPEND LONG, LONELY HOURS AT DRAWING BOARDS, SOON HEAR THEIR CHARACTERS TALKING BACK AT 'EM. USUALLY I LISTEN, EVEN RESPOND. IT'S A CUT ABOVE TALKING TO YOURSELF.

PERSONALLY, I CONSIDER DOLLARS MORE IMPORTANT THAN **SIGNS**. I WISH QUEEN ISABELLA HAD DOLLARS. DID YOU EVER TRY TO BUY 3 SHIPS WITH A MESS OF JEWELRY.

SEE PAGES 28 AND 79

...AND DON'T TELL ME ABOUT **OLIVER POLLOCK**. I'M THE ORIGINAL FORGOTTEN MAN— **AMERIGO VESPUCCI** SAW TO **THAT**

GEE! BUT THE THINGS LEFT OUT... I TOLD COLUMBUS I DIDN'T EVEN MENTION LOUISIANA'S OIL & GAS, THE OFFSHORE, THE SUPER DOME, AND SUPER PORT, SO MANY THINGS. BUT I RAN OUT OF SPACE. "WHAT WOULD YOU DO," I ASKED? AND COLUMBUS REPLIED...

I MADE FOUR TRIPS!

SO LONG AGAIN... CHASE

SECRET WEAPON

ONLY AMONG THE ANGLO-AMERICANS WAS WINNING THE FRONTIER A FAMILY AFFAIR... SCULPTOR O'NEIL'S "PIONEER WOMAN" REVEALS THE RESOLUTE WIFE AND MOTHER WHO SHARED HER MAN'S TRIUMPH IN MAKING A WILDERNESS THEIR HOME... AND OUR NATION.

WITHOUT THESE TWO REDHEADS, **JEFFERSON** AND **POLLOCK**, THIS STORY COULDN'T HAVE BEEN TOLD. THERE WOULD NOT HAVE BEEN ANY **LOUISIANA PURCHASE.**

Her Headquarters
A CABIN IN A CLEARING

WITHOUT THE GUIDANCE OF AN INDIAN PRINCESS (SEE PAGES 65-67), THE SUCCESS OF LEWIS & CLARK WAS DOUBTFULL. OREGON, WASHINGTON & IDAHO ARE U.S. STATES DUE TO THIS EXPEDITION WHICH COST $2,500. THE LOUISIANA PURCHASE GOT ABOUT 15 STATES, BUT HAD TO PAY $1,000,000 FOR EACH!

SACAGAWEA (ABOVE) HAD BEEN CAPTURED AND ENSLAVED. ONLY BY ACCIDENT WERE HER SERVICES ACQUIRED, AS WERE **YORK'S**, A HUGE BLACK MAN, SLAVE OF CLARK. HE SO IMPRESSED THE INDIANS THEY STAYED PEACEFULL

—**LATER**... FREED BY CLARK-**YORK** RETURNED WEST, WHERE THE INDIANS MADE HIM A **CHIEF**!

FOR THE "SECRET WEAPON" IN ACTION—SEE PAGES 20-21.

ABOUT THE AUTHOR

"Have you ever done a self-portrait?" John Churchill Chase allowed he had done one, once. It captures Chase the observer of people and events: the man with an eye for the whimsy of it all.

The first artist, it seems, to crop up in his English, Scotch-Irish and French family tree, Chase was born in New Orleans and educated at several public schools, St. Stanislaus and Newman, then went on to the Chicago Academy of Fine Arts. He spent a year in Chicago on the *Gasoline Alley* comic strip, then returned home as editorial cartoonist for *The Morning Tribune, Item, Times-Picayune* and *States,* and *States-Item.*

Next, Chase originated the television editorial cartoon for NBC's New Orleans affiliate, WDSU-TV. The format was later adopted by many stations around the country.

His credits include five books (six if you count *Of Time and Chase,* a collection edited by Edison B. Allen) not counting many guidebooks and illustrating works by other Louisiana authors. Chase has originated historical cartoon murals for three New Orleans buildings; was historian for *Musee Conti,* the New Orleans Wax Museum; designed a stained glass window ("Christ at the Transfiguration") for St. Dominic's Church, New Orleans; lectured on New Orleans history at Tulane for some thirty years; taught editorial cartooning on educational television and in person at UNO.

Past president of the Association of Editorial Cartoonists, Chase also was a founding member of the National Cartoonists Society, a founding member of International House and a founding father of Escargot Gourmet Society. He also claims to be the undefeated, undisputed duelling champion of New Orleans, all because he wields the *epee* with his cartooning hand (the left one).

Other Pelican Titles of Interest

200 YEARS OF NEW ORLEANS COOKING
By Natalie V. Scott
Decorations by William Spratling
Savory recipes from New Orleans kitchens gathered from the past 200 years.
ISBN: 1-56554-441-2 $15.95 pb (F)

BELIZAIRE THE CAJUN
By Glen Pitre
Edited by Dean Shapiro
This historical novel, based on the 1986 motion picture, recounts the exploits of Belizaire Breaux, a Cajun herbalist and *traiteur* (faith healer).
ISBN: 0-88289-671-7 $10.95 pb (F)

BERNARDO DE GALVEZ IN LOUISIANA: 1776-1793
By John Walton Caughey
Foreword by Jack D. L. Holmes
Appointed governor in 1776 at the age of thirty, Galvez was one of the most able colonial governors. Covers events during the six pivotal years that helped shape the destiny of frontier Louisiana.
ISBN: 1-56554-517-6 $19.95 pb (F)

CABANOCEY
   The History, Customs, and Folklore of St. James Parish
By Lillian C. Bourgeois
Classic account of how the people of St. James Parish lived, who they were, and what they contributed to their society over a hundred years ago.
ISBN: 1-56554-518-4 $24.00 pb (F)

CAVALIER IN THE WILDERNESS
By Ross Phares
Illustrated by Jack Hastings
For a large part of the first half of the eighteenth century, Louis Juchereau de St. Denis was the guiding force on the Louisiana-Texas frontier.
ISBN: 0-88289-127-8 $24.00 pb (F)

THE BLACK HILLS
By Lt. Col. Richard Irving Dodge
An early account of the exploration of the Black Hills in the Rocky Mountains, on one of the U.S. military's first scientific journeys of discovery.
ISBN: 1-56554-573-7 $14.95 pb (F)

THE CABILDO ON JACKSON SQUARE
By Samuel Wilson, Jr. and Leonard V. Huber
The Cabildo is undoubtedly the most important surviving monument of the period of Spanish domination in Louisiana. This volume traces the history of the Cabildo from its construction in 1769.
ISBN: 0-911116-41-9 $14.95 pb (F)

CHILDREN OF STRANGERS
By Lyle Saxon
A powerful and moving story of love in a community bound by race and class on Melrose Plantation on the Cane River.
ISBN: 0-88289-397-1 $12.95 pb

FABULOUS NEW ORLEANS
By Lyle Saxon
This classic reprint evokes a city steeped in the traditions and idiosyncrasies of three cultures—French, Spanish, and American. By any standards, New Orleans is a unique city, and Saxon depicts it unadorned, with all its flaws and glories.
ISBN: 0-88289-706-3 $12.95 pb

FATHER MISSISSIPPI
By Lyle Saxon
The story of the great Mississippi River flood of 1927, with photos.
ISBN: 1-56554-795-0 $30.00 pb (F)

LAFITTE THE PIRATE
By Lyle Saxon
No fictional swashbuckler could ever rival Jean Lafitte's dramatic life. A superbly written account examines Lafitte's fascinating career and frees the truth of the pirate's life from the web of fantastic myths that grew around him.
ISBN: 0-88289-395-5 $14.95 pb

OLD LOUISIANA
By Lyle Saxon
A fascinating volume, *Old Louisiana* chronicles much of the state's history. Vignettes depict the early French settlers, the later Spanish rulers, and the rise and collapse of the plantation era.
ISBN: 0-88289-705-5 $12.95 pb

THE CONQUEST OF THE MISSOURI
By Joseph Mills Hanson
The 1909 story of the opening of the Northwest told from the perspective of Capt. Grant Marsh, who helped survey the upper reaches of the Missouri and pioneered steamboat travel to the area.
ISBN: 1-58980-064-8 $12.95 pb

FLAGS OF LOUISIANA
By Jeanne Frois
Illustrated by Larry Pardue
The story behind the exchange of governmental power, as well as the symbols of each flag.
ISBN: 1-56554-047-6 $16.95

THE FRENCH IN THE HEART OF AMERICA
By John Finley
The French settlers traveled throughout much of the New World claiming land for their country. Their journey through the valley of the St. Lawrence River, around the Great Lakes, in the Mississippi Valley to ultimately reach the Gulf of Mexico.
ISBN: 1-56554-448-X $25.00 pb (F)

FRENCHMEN, DESIRE, GOOD CHILDREN
   . . . and Other Streets of New Orleans!
By John Churchill Chase
The interesting stories of the infamous and famous people, places, and events from which the city's names and character are drawn.
ISBN: 1-56554-931-7 $16.95 pb

1-800-843-1724 or 1-888-5-PELICAN

GILBERT ANTOINE DE ST. MAXENT
The Spanish Frenchman from New Orleans
By James Julian Coleman, Jr.
A biography of a leader in colonial Louisiana. Gilbert Antoine de St. Maxent helped form a tiny outpost in the vast wilderness of upper Louisiana that would become the great city of St. Louis, Missouri.
ISBN: 0-911116-06-0 $19.95

THE GRANDISSIMES
By George Washington Cable
Foreword by W. Kenneth Holditch
The best book on Creole life. The novel has been considered a masterful critique of racial and social inequality that resonates with readers even today.
ISBN: 1-56554-901-5 $7.99 pb

GUMBO YA-YA: Folk Tales of Louisiana
By Lyle Saxon, Edward Dreyer, and Robert Tallant
Long considered the finest collection of Louisiana folk tales and customs, *Gumbo Ya-Ya* chronicles the stories and legends that have emerged from the bayou country.
ISBN: 0-88289-645-8 $17.95 pb

THE HAUNTING OF LOUISIANA
By Barbara Sillery
Based on the PBS documentary. Louisiana's haunted reputation is spotlighted in the twenty chapters that cover the ghostly escapades and happenings at Oak Alley Plantation, Ormond Plantation, Destrehan Manor, and America's "most haunted home": The Myrtles, in St. Francisville.
ISBN: 1-56554-905-8 $17.95 pb

THE INDIANS OF LOUISIANA
By Fred B. Kniffen
Illustrated by Mildred Compton
Traces the journeys of the first Indians to arrive in Louisiana more than a thousand years ago and provides a general overview of their cultures.
ISBN: 0-911116-97-4 $14.95

LOUISIANA PURCHASE: An American Story
Written and illustrated by John Chase
A complete and detailed history of this vast territory and its transfer to the United States told in comic-book format.
ISBN: 1-58980-084-0 $12.95 pb

NO MAN'S LAND: A History of El Camino Real
By Louis R. Nardini
In America, the El Camino Real was an important road that began in Mexico City, where the king's representative would be, and ended at the north end of Front Street in Natchitoches, Louisiana. This is the record of it.
ISBN: 1-56554-611-3 $19.95 pb (F)

PLANTATION LIFE ON THE MISSISSIPPI
By W. E. Clement
Provides an in-depth look at daily plantation life in Reconstruction-era Louisiana. Personal reminiscences of the author's boyhood on a sugar plantation are intermingled with colorful character portraits of local citizens.
ISBN: 1-56554-436-6 $16.95 pb (F)

SOCIAL LIFE IN OLD NEW ORLEANS
By Eliza Ripley
Ms. Ripley takes readers back to antebellum days in New Orleans, describing everything from boarding school to old wedding traditions.
ISBN: 1-56554-460-9 $19.95 pb (F)

THE SPANISH IN NEW ORLEANS AND LOUISIANA
By José Montero de Pedro, Marqués de Casa Mena
Translated by Richard E. Chandler
The all-too-recognizable French influences of Creole and Cajun culture in Louisiana and New Orleans make way for an examination of the effects of the Spanish period, which lasted from 1763 to 1803.
ISBN: 1-56554-685-7 $24.95

TALES OF THE MISSISSIPPI
By Ray Samuel, Leonard V. Huber, and Warren C. Ogden
Over 300 magnificent pictures and rollicking tales about Old Man River. Rafts, keelboats, flatboats, side-wheelers, sternwheelers, snagboats, steamboats, gunboats, showboats--all provided a stage for the cast of legendary characters.
ISBN: 0-88289-930-9 $19.95 pb

VOYAGE TO LOUISIANA, 1803-1805
By C. C. Robin
Translated by Stuart O. Landry, Jr.
Robin's adventures in 1803 that took him to Pensacola, New Orleans, and the Attakapas and Ouachita country.
ISBN: 1-56554-571-0 $25.00 pb (F)

HISTORIC WASHINGTON, ARKANSAS
By Steven Brooke
An in-depth look at the architecture of Old Washington including its courthouse, schools, taverns, churches, working print shop, and a weapons museum. The most important Arkansas city in 1830.
ISBN: 1-56554-652-0 $9.95 pb

WE ARE ACADIANS
Nous Sommes Acadiens
By Myron Tassin
A pictorial essay portraying the many faces of the timeless Cajuns of Louisiana.
ISBN: 0-88289-117-0 $8.95

EVANGELINE
By Henry Wadsworth Longfellow
Edited by Lewis B. Semple
Foreword by Henri-Dominique Paratte
The heartbreaking story of two Acadian lovers separated during the expulsion of the French settlers from Nova Scotia. The story is enhanced by the new foreword by Henri-Dominique Paratte.
ISBN: 1-56554-474-9 $6.95 pb

ROUSSEAU: The Last Days of Spanish New Orleans
By Raymond J. Martinez
The activities of Pierre George Rousseau, Louisiana's naval hero who held the post of commanding general of the galleys of the Mississippi under six Spanish governors of Louisiana. Also provides well-researched sketches of each of the Spanish governors of Louisiana, along with vivid glimpses of social life in New Orleans.
ISBN: 1-58980-089-3 $14.95 pb (F)